Conversation in the Spirit:

A Guide to the
Synodal Method

Juan A. Guerrero Alves SJ
& Óscar Martín López SJ

With a prologue by Pope Francis
Translated by Austen Ivereigh

Translated by Austen Ivereigh

Published by Messenger Publications, 2025

ISBN: 9781788127288

Designed by Brendan McCarthy
Typeset in Garamond Premier Pro
Printed by Hussar Books

Messenger MJP Publications

Messenger Publications,
Milltown Park, Dublin D06 W9Y7, Ireland
www.messenger.ie

Contents

4

Adsumus, Sancte Spiritus[1]

We stand before you, Holy Spirit,
as we gather together in your name.
With you alone to guide us,
make yourself at home in our hearts;
teach us the way we must go,
and how we are to pursue it.
We are weak and sinful;
do not let us promote disorder.
Do not let ignorance lead us down the wrong path
nor partiality influence our actions.
Let us find in you our unity
so that we may journey together to eternal life
and not stray from the way of truth
and what is right.
All this we ask of you,
who are at work in every place and time,
in the communion of the Father and the Son,
forever and ever. Amen.

---

1   Prayer invoking the Holy Spirit for an ecclesial assembly of governance of discernment, that is, any synodal meeting (see www.synod.va). Each session of the Second Vatican Council began with the 'Adsumus, Sancte Spiritus' prayer, the title of which comes from the first line of the prayer 'We stand before you, Holy Spirit'. The prayer has been used historically in councils, synods and other gatherings of the Church over many centuries and is attributed to St Isidore of Seville (560–636).

Prologue

Vatican, 21 July 2023

Dear brothers:

Thank you for sharing with me this book prior to its publication. As you tell the story behind it in your introduction, I see that Óscar has succeeded in wresting his colleague from the world of economics in which we had trapped him in this house, returning him to more spiritual topics.[2] How beautiful that from the spiritual conversation of the two authors has been born a book on conversation in the Spirit.

Although conversation in the Spirit – the method adopted on the synodal pathway – is the main subject of the book, I am glad that you go beyond the method and how it works. I note with satisfaction that you supply historical reference points to allow the reader to capture the depth of the method and all that it brings into play, so that it becomes truly an experience of listening to the Spirit. You highlight how the synodal method is above all a spiritual experience, in which speaking and listening seek to allow the Holy Spirit to be the true protagonist. As we follow the thread of the book, we become aware that the synodal journey we have undertaken is truly an experience of the Spirit – personally, communally and as a Church – that demands of each individual, therefore, interior work.

The idea of conversation as 'pouring into the same common channel' deserves further development. Understanding conversation in this way allows each person to offer his or her point of view to enrich that common channel. How much good it would do us to have a greater measure

---

2 **Translator's note**: Fr Juan Guerrero Alves SJ served as prefect of the Vatican's Secretariat for the Economy from 1 January 2020 to 30 November 2022.

of conversation in civic and church life! In conversation in the Spirit we find a way of taking part that builds up communion and renews mission, which encourages the participation of all and which welcomes our great diversity in communion and unity.

Conversation in the Spirit, discernment and synodality consist, more than anything, in listening. The synodal way that the Church has undertaken is a path of deep listening. What you propose is fundamental and much needed: 'an open and vulnerable listening', one that allows the Spirit to move and change us, allowing us to choose and to act on our choices. If everyone remains entrenched in the positions they already hold, there will not be a true conversation nor a true listening to the Spirit. They will find nothing to learn or to take on board from others. And they will be afraid of any choice that implies change. For only when we truly listen, will we come out richer and can deepen communion and mission.

The chapter on interior dispositions strikes me as especially necessary. As I have said on more than one occasion, we are not summoning a parliament nor carrying out an opinion survey. We want to walk together as brothers and sisters, listening to the Holy Spirit. The Spirit is the true protagonist of the synod. Listening to the Spirit demands of us a particular interior disposition. Conversation in the Spirit, discernment and synodality can only advance if we empty ourselves in order to be filled with the Spirit. Only if our freedom is set free from material, ideological and emotional attachments will we let the Spirit lead us more effectively. Only by cultivating interior attitudes of humility, hospitality and welcome, while at the same time banishing all self-sufficiency and self-referentiality, will our communion and mission be strengthened.

You dedicate the final chapter to the concrete way of carrying out a conversation in the Spirit, explaining the method, how to put it into practice and the aspects that need particular attention. This chapter shouldn't be read as if it were the conclusion of the book. Every method is a means to an end, not the end itself. The synod documents themselves refer to needing to adapt the method to different situations so that it is genuinely useful. The importance of the earlier chapters is precisely that they allow the methodology to be properly prepared and applied.

The synod's *Final Document* speaks of the need for formation in conversation in the Spirit. I believe that the book you are presenting provides valuable materials for that purpose. I thank you for your efforts; I am sure it will prove an excellent aid in many church contexts.

May Jesus bless you and the Virgin care for you and please: don't forget to pray for me,

Francis,

Francisco

Introduction

In October 2021, Pope Francis opened the so-called 'Synod on Synodality', inviting us to 'walk together', led by the Spirit, in a Church that across the world faces very different challenges yet also many in common.[3] Each particular Church has its own context. But if there is an element common to all the contexts in which the Church is present, it is the polarisation of our societies. Ever sharper divisions make it seemingly impossible to row together in the same direction in search of the common good. Bonds of social friendship are weaker, the reconciliation of different standpoints harder, and to converse seeking the common good seems a distant, even impossible goal. Many open discussions and debates in our societies appear at times incapable of reaching shared solutions. What we lack are conversations on important questions to which everyone brings their perspective in order to enrich the world we share in common.

It is precisely the instrument of conversation in the Spirit that prevents polarisation and creates harmony; the synod has used it to enable the participation of all to contribute to communion and mission. As the synod's handbook puts it, 'this journey together not only unites us more deeply with one another as the People of God, it also sends us out to pursue our mission as a prophetic witness that embraces the entire family of humanity, together with our fellow Christian denominations and other faith traditions.'[4]

---

3 Pope Francis, 'Address of the Holy Father Francis on the Occasion of the Moment of Reflection for the Beginning of the Synodal Journey', bulletin, 9 October 2021, https://press.vatican.va/content/salastampa/en/bollettino/pubblico/2021/10/09/211009a.html. There is a brief description of the various elements in common and difficulties faced by the Church today in the so-called *Vademecum* or official handbook for listening and discernment by local Churches in the first phase of the Synod on Synodality.
4 Secretary General of the Synod of Bishops, *Vademecum for the Synod on Synodality* (Synod of Bishops, 2021), 1, www.synod.va/en/news/the-vademecum-for-the-synod-on-synodality.html

The importance of conversation in the Spirit as the key synodal method has become ever clearer as the process has developed. In June 2023 the *Instrumentum Laboris*, or working document, was drawn up for the first of the two concluding assemblies in Rome the following October. The *Instrumentum Laboris* developed the notion of conversation in the Spirit in a whole section (paras 32–42), defining it as 'a shared prayer with a view to communal discernment for which participants prepare themselves by personal reflection and meditation'. The *Instrumentum Laboris* noted how important the method had been to the diocesan and continental phases of the synod, and how in some instances it was called 'spiritual conversation' in others 'conversation in the Spirit' or simply 'the synodal method'. [5] All three expressions refer to the same thing and can be used – as we will in this book – interchangeably.

Following the experience of using conversation in the Spirit during the three weeks of that assembly, the synod members embraced it enthusiastically in their concluding *Synthesis Report* of October 2023 and called for it to be adopted across the Church. The following June 2024, the *Instrumentum Laboris* for the second session quoted the regional episcopal body FABC that across Asia the Church had incorporated the method into their existing structures 'with great success', adding later that conversation in the Spirit was 'particularly well suited to the exercise of synodality'.[6] In their *Synthesis Report*, the synod members said its use 'avoided us moving too quickly to a debate based on the reiteration of our own positions without listening first to the reasoning that supports the position of others'.[7] In October 2024 the *Final Document* summed up the experience of using the method over the three-year journey:

> Conversation in the Spirit is a tool that, even with its limitations, enables listening in order to discern 'what the Spirit is saying to the Churches' (Rev 2:7). Its practice has

---

5 *Instrumentum Laboris for the First Session* (Synod of Bishops, 2023), 37, www.synod.va/content/dam/synod/common/phases/universal-stage/il/ENG_INSTRUMENTUM-LABORIS.pdf

6 *Instrumentum Laboris for the Second Session* (Synod of Bishops, 2024), 65, www.synod.va/content/dam/synod/assembly2024/il/ENG-INSTRUMENTUM-LABORIS-A4.pdf

7 *Synthesis Report* (Synod of Bishops, 2023), 15a, www.synod.va/en/news/a-synodal-church-in-mission.html

elicited joy, awe and gratitude and has been experienced as a path of renewal that transforms individuals, groups and the Church. The word 'conversation' expresses more than mere dialogue: it interweaves thought and feeling, creating a shared vital space. That is why we can say that conversion is at play in conversation. This is an anthropological reality found in different peoples and cultures, who gather together in solidarity to deal with and decide matters vital to the community. Grace brings this human experience to fruition. Conversing 'in the Spirit' means living the experience of sharing in the light of faith and seeking God's will in an evangelical atmosphere within which the Holy Spirit's unmistakable voice can be heard.[8]

So we have here a methodology that enables all to participate in the service of the Church's communion and mission, one that has proved itself hugely helpful for opening up channels of communication and discernment within the Church. A methodology, furthermore, that has allowed a greater number than ever of believers to contribute to the Church what the Spirit is offering through them. What spiritual conversation makes evident is the desire for encounter in the Church characterised by the dynamism of the Holy Spirit, a way of interacting and discerning that seeks truth in love and listens attentively to the different voices present in the People of God. In this way, it has enabled a greater openness to other realities and challenges. This has been of great help in discernment processes, which have in turn showed the need of reforms in the different areas of church life.

The *Final Document* of the synod process places great stress on the need of formation of all the baptised in order to engage in decision-making grounded in ecclesial discernment, a formation that is not only technical but also has theological, biblical and spiritual foundations.[9] Ecclesial discernment is above all 'a spiritual practice grounded in a living faith' that

8 *Final Document* (Synod of Bishops, 2024), 45, www.synod.va/content/dam/synod/news/2024-10-26_final-document/ENG---Documento-finale.pdf

9 *Final Document*, 80.

calls for 'interior freedom, humility, prayer, mutual trust, an openness to the new and a surrender to the will of God'. It is an invitation to everyone, for 'the more everyone is heard, the richer the discernment'.

The method of spiritual conversation is key to this: 'Each person, speaking according to their conscience, is called to open themselves to the others, who share according to their conscience.'[10] In this sharing, they come to perceive what the Spirit is saying to the Church. The *Instrumentum Laboris* describes formation in conversation in the Spirit as 'a priority at all levels of ecclesial life', adding that 'formation in conversation in the Spirit is formation to be a synodal Church'.[11] In the pages that follow we want to contribute to that formation, helping people understand and apply the method while at the same time deepening the spiritual dispositions it calls for, which allow for the Spirit to be the true protagonist of the synodal method.

As Jesuits, we authors are most familiar with the Ignatian tradition, which we will refer to often in introducing the reader into spiritual conversation. But we are very aware that in other spiritual traditions, both before and after St Ignatius, there are similar modalities, or at least ways that fulfil the same purpose of building communion and defining mission. Discernment and spiritual conversation have been part of the spiritual tradition of the Church from its first centuries. Because this is an instrument to be used by different people in varying contexts and spaces in the Church, the synod documents sensibly warn against being too rigid in applying the method and call for 'appropriate adaptation' to the different circumstances and needs.[12] Conversation in the Spirit classically has three phases or 'rounds', but there may be occasions, for example, when one of the three rounds needs to be emphasised or take priority over the others. But even keeping in mind the need for these occasional adjustments, 'the intention and dynamism that unite the three steps are and remain characteristic of the way of proceeding of a synodal Church'.[13]

In addition to the methodological aspects, the questions that Pope Francis left us in his homily at the Mass celebrated at the synod's launch

10 *Final Document*, 82.
11 *Instrumentum Laboris for the First Session*, 42.
12 *Final Document*, 10.
13 *Instrumentum Laboris for the First Session*, 41.

are important. They are questions that point us to what is essential in the process, which is not concerned only with matters internal to the Church but goes to the heart of her mission. For the Holy Father, the Synod on Synodality has as its objectives encounter, listening, discernment and interior transformation – at every level of the Church. 'The Gospels frequently show us Jesus "on a journey"; he walks alongside people and listens to the questions and concerns lurking in their hearts. He shows us that God is not found in neat and orderly places, distant from reality, but walks ever at our side. He meets us where we are, on the often rocky roads of life.' The Holy Father went on to ask 'whether we, the Christian community, embody this "style" of God, who travels the paths of history and shares in the life of humanity. Are we prepared for the adventure of this journey? Or are we fearful of the unknown, preferring to take refuge in the usual excuses: "It's no use" or "We've always done it this way"?'[14]

Synodality is not an event or slogan but a style, a way of being with which the Church wishes to live its mission in the world. It is the whole People of God that must take that mission forward, not just a part of it. It is up to all the members of the church body to set off on this road, each of us with our gifts and charisms, serving each in our different ways, united to each other as in a single body. A synodal Church walks together in communion in pursuit of a common mission, and in that mission all its members play a part. In these pages you will find the means for every member to contribute to the Church in ways that allow their interior dispositions to create space for what the Spirit is saying to the Church as a whole.

When the People of God sets off on a journey, some go faster than others, like the disciples John and Peter when they ran to the Lord's tomb (Jn 20:4–8). In our synodal process, in which the whole Church is journeying together, people go at different speeds. Some, urged on by the call they feel and the need they perceive, want quickly to move ahead. Others, concerned to get everything right, want to go slower and more carefully. When there are many of us moving ahead together, like those who walked

---

14 Pope Francis, 'Homily of His Holiness Pope Francis at the Opening of the Synodal Path', multimedia, 10 October 2021, www.vatican.va/content/francesco/en/homilies/2021/documents/20211010-omelia-sinodo-vescovi.html

through the desert, both attitudes are particularly desirable: that of John, who holds back, as well as that of Peter, who rushes ahead. It is important to keep in the mind the importance of this 'exodus discipline' such that, while the people are stretched, they do not break apart.

The story and structure of this book

Óscar Martín is part of a team named by the Paraguayan bishops' conference to promote and accompany the synodal process in the dioceses of that country. In that role he has often used, as recommended, the spiritual conversation method to enable the sharing and discernment that build communion. During his involvement in the synod's continental stage, at the assembly of the Southern Cone in the Brazilian capital, Brasilia, some bishops urged him to write a book about spiritual conversation, which was proving very fruitful in the synod process, to help their communities and dioceses. It happened that, in those months, Juan Antonio Guerrero was staying in the same Jesuit community as Óscar, in the 'Holy Martyrs' Spirituality Centre in the Paraguayan capital, Asunción. Juan Antonio was dedicating time to prayer and the study of spiritual themes. The spiritual conversations that the two of us had over those months meant that the request made to Óscar ended up being received by both of us. Having shared much of the contents of this book in those conversations, we decided to write it together.

In presenting spiritual conversation, we will enter into the subject through seven 'moments'.

Moment One

We distinguish the action of conversing from other ways of communicating, while introducing a brief reflection on the importance of conversation in civic life, noting how the absence of it is leading our societies down the routes of polarisation and disorientation in the search for truth and the common good.

Moment Two

We try to relate spiritual conversation to the synodal conversion the Church is now called to undertake.

Moment Three
We link spiritual conversation to processes of discernment and decision-making in groups, using the famous example of the deliberations of the first Jesuits in 1539, which seems to us a paradigmatic example of spiritual conversation geared to a communal discernment.

Moment Four
We pause to describe ways of sharing and listening that are appropriate to conversations in the Spirit.

Moment Five
We consider the prior spiritual dispositions of those taking part, which are the precondition *sine qua non* of communion and discernment in common.

Moment Six
We pause to reflect, offering some theological points on spiritual conversation, discernment and synodality.

Moment Seven
We turn to the proper preparation of a spiritual conversation, whether or not it is aimed at discerning a decision: that is, the method to follow, the role of the facilitator, and how to create space for listening to the Spirit to strengthen communion and shed light on mission.

We end with an appendix outlining a series of practical guidelines for holding a spiritual conversation and a discernment in common, as well as biblical passages that can shed light on different moments in a spiritual conversation.

Moment One:
From Conversation to Spiritual Conversation

It is a curious fact that when two friends speak together in some countries they call it *conversing* and in others *discussing*. Normally these mean the same thing, but the words have different connotations. At times we will use the terms indistinctly, as synonyms of *dialogue* and *debate*. But we will use the word *dispute* much less often. In reality, all these words have different etymologies and have been used differently at different times in the past. Let's briefly review them to understand better the nuances of each word.

Disputation normally has a competitive connotation. In the dictionary definition its first meaning is to debate or discourse argumentatively; a second refers to challenging a point of view or claim; while a third is to contend with opposing arguments or assertions.[15] *Dispute* comes from the Latin *dis-* (separation) and *putāre* (to think). In philosophy we used to refer to 'disputed questions' (the title of a work by St Thomas Aquinas): in metaphysical disputations two contenders argued from reason, making their cases, and one of them would win. Disputes can be understood as divergences in thinking and have their context, rules and themes. Disputing is not conversing.

---

15 **Translator's note**: the authors, citing the authoritative Spanish dictionary of the Royal Academy, add another definition, 'to strive or struggle', which in English is now obsolete according to the *Oxford English Dictionary* (*OED*). In the definitions and etymologies in this section I have followed where possible the *OED*.

Debate similarly has a competitive connotation. In a debate there is normally a winner and a loser. The word comes from the Latin *debattuĕre* (to beat, shake or churn). Used of two or more people, the dictionary defines it as discussing a theme with different opinions. Debating is not conversing either.

Discussion uses the particle *dis-* (denial or contrariness) and derives from the Latin *discutere* (to shake violently or to scatter). It means to determine a matter by pitting one thing against another, to have them compete. Discussing too has a competitive purpose: two subjects, each seeking to overcome the other by having their arguments triumph. Each has its perspective, its point of view to defend, and the fact that one wins implies necessarily that the other loses. If the winner not only overcomes the other but convinces his audience, he will earn himself allies, disciples and followers, but they will not be on an equal footing to him.

Dialogue for the ancient Greeks referred to the process of knowing by means of speech or writing. The word is made up of the Greek prefix *dia-* (by means of) and *logos* (word, logic, knowledge). Plato used dialogues to arrive at the truth by means of the word: reason and logic. Those who dialogued, starting from differing presuppositions, reached a common conclusion or a meeting point. In dialogue it is possible for one of the dialogue partners to convince the other. But it can also happen that each simply understands the other, respecting their different presuppositions. Although certainly of great value in all circumstances of our lives, we have to say that dialoguing, too, is not the same as conversing. In dialogue what is missing is a common channel.

The synod's handbook stresses the importance of dialogue in the context of the synod. It says that dialogue requires perseverance and patience and adds: 'The dialogue between Christians of different confessions, united by one baptism, has a special place in the synodal journey.'[16]

Conversing: etymologically, *con-* means 'meeting', 'aggregation' or 'corporation', while the Latin *versare* means 'to go around'. As well as meaning 'people talking with each other', there are a couple of largely obsolete meanings of interest. One is 'to associate familiarly, keep company with';

16 *Vademecum*, 5.3: 6, 7.

another is 'to commune with'. So what these approximations make clear is that the purpose of conversation is *cooperative*: that is, all who engage in it are able to win; and all share a world, collaborate or join together in exploring a theme. Using another image, we can say that *con-versing* is like a pouring together into a common stream or watercourse, transforming individuals into community. As the *Final Document* puts it, 'conversion is at play in conversation'.[17]

Conversation creates friendship: civic friendship, social friendship or just plain friendship. We can verify this from different perspectives. In his encyclical *Fratelli Tutti*, for example, the Holy Father invites us to go deeply into social friendship and fraternity. For Aristotle, friendship is 'the most necessary thing for life. Without friends no one would want to live ... Young people need [friends] in order to avoid mistakes, old people because they need help ... those in the flower of their lives [need friends] for noble actions: "two walking together" are, in reality, more capable of thinking and acting.'[18] For the Greek philosopher, friendship holds cities together because in them common purposes are shared. Friends share a common good; they inhabit a common world while having different perspectives on it. It is not, as some authors claim, simply about having shared feelings, the same point of view or the same theories.[19]

Conversation in civic life

There is a glaring lack of conversation in our civic life. A much-discussed recent book on the deterioration of democracies speaks of the 'three Ps': populism, polarisation and post-truth.[20] Populism is not so much an ideology as a strategy for gaining and exercising power. The populist will say what others want to hear with the aim of gaining power, without the need of acting later on his pledges.

Polarisation seeks to create groups or parties that are strongly radicalised around certain themes: social, political, economic, religious etc. One

---

17 *Final Document*, 45.
18 Aristotle, *Etica a Nicomaco* (Madrid: Centro de Estudios Políticos y Constitucionales, 2009), 1155a, 122.
19 For example, J. Rawls, *Teoría de la justicia* (México: FCE, 1985), pp. 5, 517, 536, 572.
20 M. Naim, *La revancha de los poderosos: Cómo los autócratas están reinventando la política del siglo XXI* (Barcelona: Debate, 2022).

of the most common strategies is to demonise those who think differently, to paint them as adversaries. Normally, the topics are present-day, but the past, too, can be fought over. The aim is always to separate and divide society, to accentuate differences. Often this leads to fanaticism, which makes it practically impossible to have a constructive, mutually enriching dialogue or peaceful conversation, one that allows different viewpoints to be offered to build a better world which, in reality, all share. This social reality has at times sadly contaminated the Church.

Post-truth goes far beyond simple lying, which, of course, has always been present in civic life. The novelty and gravity of post-truth is in the fact that those who promote it do not limit themselves to promoting lies but rather deny from the outset the very notion of an independent reality that is verifiable. It's not just about accepting falsehoods as truths but about muddying the waters to the point where it is hard or even impossible to distinguish between truth and falsehood. Truth itself is scorned, or, what is worse, turned into what each faction or splinter group defends, whether through fake news, data manipulation or by repeating half-truths, always in an attempt to turn things to their own advantage.

The accelerating deterioration of civic life in our society is an observable fact. And authors are not lacking who have foreseen it, at least since the 1960s. One was Hannah Arendt, who already at that time saw the decline in the public sphere along with the loss of a 'common world', a space in which shared human problems could be resolved. For Arendt, this was a space in which common problems could be dealt with either competitively or collaboratively, depending on the nature of the problems.

Seeking to shed light on this reality, a number of authors who have studied this deterioration in public or civic life have highlighted an important element: the loss of spaces that traditionally hosted conversation, spaces where all can bring their perspectives and opinions to bear on common themes. In the 1990s Christopher Lasch wrote,

> If the elites speak only to themselves, it is also because there
> do not exist institutions that promote general conversation
> beyond the boundaries of class. Civic life calls for environ-
> ments where people can meet as equals, independently of

their race, class or national origin. Yet now, thanks to the decline of civic institutions, from political parties to public parks to informal meeting places, conversation has become no less sectoral than the production of knowledge. The social classes speak among themselves in their own slang, inaccessible to outsiders; they come together only on occasional ceremonial occasions or on official feasts.[21]

The North-American sociologist Ray Oldenburg reclaims what he calls 'third places', meaning intermediate meeting spaces between, on the one hand, the family, and, on the other, our professional roles and the big structures in which we work.[22] Without those environments, says the author, the city simply becomes a desert. Among those spaces are typically the bar, the barber's, the shop, the neighbourhood street, the square, the sports' club, and so on. These third places take the pressure off the family, an institution which, nowadays, we ask too much of as the only alternative space to the workplace.

This so-called 'third space' is the space of conversation. It is there that we create the common channel into which the participation of all is poured. There certain topics recur that flow from a shared world, held in common. Models of excellence emerge, depending on what is being praised or rejected in the conversation. A shared identity comes into being that progressively makes space for others.

Conversation is the great protagonist of 'third spaces', which are generally informal and without great pretensions. In them we see individual characteristics and the richness of each personality being expressed. At its most basic, conversation serves the basic human need for communion. For those who watch them from afar, people in conversation seem more in tune with each other than they are in reality. What they have in common is the topic that brings them together. But the individuals are very different, as are their different perspectives and what they bring to the

---

21   C. Lasch, *La rebelión de las élites y la traición a la democracia* (Barcelona: Paidos, 1996). The whole of his chapter 6 is relevant to our theme.
22   R. Oldenburg, *The Great Good Place: Cafes, Coffee Shops, Community Centers, Beauty Parlors, General Stores, Bars, Hangouts and How They Get You through the Day* (New York: Marlow & Co, 1997).

conversation.

Another quality of conversation is that it generates a space of equality: it is levelling by nature. Questions such as social class, status or worldly rank are left outside the door. Also left outside the conversation are personal problems, people's moods and so on. In this way, conversation enables encounter between different people on an equal footing. In that equality we can glimpse a larger world, beyond that of friends and family.

Conversation also has an integrating quality: it brings different people together and creates a common language. In our society, by contrast, it is very normal for classes and social groups to speak their own dialects, incomprehensible to others. If we are not careful, the common language is gradually lost, and each group will work only with its own jargon.

In contrast, conversation creates an encounter we might call non-functional. In this space we meet, for example, work colleagues in a more complete and true way than the workplace allows. In this gratuitous encounter that generates conversation new horizons can open spontaneously; we discover people's hobbies, gifts and virtues. Conversation allows us to leave aside functions and roles. People relate to each other without rules other than those of 'decency'. In spaces of conversation decency is more important than economic success or the social position one might occupy.

We can certainly say that conversation is a key indicator of the vitality of a community and is a great loss when it is disappears. What generates its atmosphere is not the place where it takes place, but the very people who converse, especially those who are regularly there. We need to take note, also, of the importance of warmly welcoming those who join later. This attitude of openness favours and broadens the conversation. Pouring into a common channel becomes a home away from home, a reference point that creates roots. To converse is to share a common world.

Spiritual conversation

We agree to call 'spiritual conversation' or 'conversation in the Spirit' a conversation in which those taking part have a deep desire to open themselves up to the Spirit in order to create fraternity, take decisions together or open up new paths under the guidance of the same Spirit. As the

Instrumentum Laboris notes, conversation in the Spirit is an expression that, in both of its terms, is heavy with meaning: *conversation* because it alludes to the capacity of the word spoken and heard to generate familiarity and draw those involved closely to each other; *in the Spirit* because it identifies the true protagonist, the Spirit, always free to blow where it wills (Jn 34:8), and the desire of those in conversation to open themselves to hear its voice. And so, as the text puts it, 'gradually the conversation between brothers and sisters in faith opens the space for a "hearing together", that is, a listening together to the voice of the Spirit'.[23]

It's about welcoming and building communion, bringing together the diversity of feelings in a common channel. It's about sharing the gift of the Spirit, because in spiritual conversation the Spirit is the true protagonist. The Holy Spirit, in the words of St Basil, 'is present in each of those ready to receive it, as if it were present to that person alone, and still it sends out his grace that is complete and sufficient for all ... Through it hearts are raised, the weak are guided and the able are brought to perfection ... [and] souls in which the Spirit dwells, illuminated by the Spirit, themselves become spiritual and send out grace to others.'[24] As St Paul teaches us, 'Now there are varieties of gifts, but the same Spirit; and there are varieties of services, but the same Lord; and there are varieties of activities, but it is the same God who activates all of them in everyone. To each is given the manifestation of the Spirit for the common good' (1 Cor 12:4–7).

Jesus not only preached the kingdom of God; as the Gospels show us, he also often used spiritual conversation in his encounters with different people. It was what he did with the Samaritan woman at the well when, gently yet firmly, he dismantled her defensive attitudes until he led her to discover the source of living water inside her (Jn 4:1–42). It is also spiritual conversation when Jesus walks with his disciples around the villages of Galilee, conversing with them about what people think about who they think he is (Lk 9:18–24); or when he converses with them about whether to go to see Lazarus, who is ill, or to stay where they are (Jn 11:7–16). We can also consider it spiritual conversation when the risen

---

23 *Instrumentum Laboris for the First Session*, 33.
24 Basil of Caesarea, *El Espíritu Santo* (Madrid: Ciudad Nueva, 1996), pp. 142–3.

Lord appears alongside Cleopas and the other disciple making their way to Emmaus: how he listens to them on the road and explains to them what the Scriptures foretold about the Messiah, until they recognise him (Lk 24:13–35). Spiritual conversation is also what Jesus holds with his friend Peter to confirm him in his love and to entrust to him the mission of shepherding his flock (Jn 21:15–23).

We also find Mary in spiritual conversation. The visit to her cousin Elizabeth is a beautiful example: the protagonist is the Spirit, who fills both women (Lk 1:39–56). The first Christian communities also made use of spiritual conversation. A good example is the Council of Jerusalem. Paul and Barnabas went up to Jerusalem to find out what the Spirit was asking of the Church in terms of welcoming Gentiles. As the Acts of the Apostles tells us, 'The apostles and the elders met together to consider this matter' (Acts 5:6).

John Cassian takes note of this, observing as follows: 'St Paul ... claims to have gone up to Jerusalem only in order to meet with the apostles and to treat in private conversation the Gospel which he preached to the nations, according to the revelation and cooperation of the Lord. This example is highly instructive. It shows us that fidelity to the rules we have drawn up for ourselves not only preserves unanimity and harmony as unchangeable, but also protects us from all the ambushes of the enemy and his diabolical illusions.'[25]

In the tradition of the Church we can also find many examples of spiritual conversation between two souls overflowing with God's love and the action of the Spirit. Among these is the well-known conversation between St Augustine shortly after his baptism and St Ambrose of Milan, the two saints alternating between the outpourings of their hearts and the verses of the *Te Deum*. Or there is the example of St Paul the hermit and St Anthony of Egypt who, finding each other in the desert, 'spent the night in praise of the divine'. Above all are the conversations between St Augustine and his mother St Monica, which Augustine describes in his-

---

25 John Cassian, *Colaciones* (Madrid: Rialp, 2019), II, XVI, XII, p. 69. For an English-language version, see Cassian, *Conferences* (Mahwah, NJ: Paulist Press, 1985).

Confessions.[26] Also well known are the conversations between St Benedict of Nursia and St Scholastica,[27] or between St Teresa of Ávila and St John of the Cross, of whom Teresa writes that 'one has to speak to Fr John of the Cross with great discretion, for if not, not only does he enter into ecstasy but causes others to do so'.[28]

These types of spiritual conversation may express spiritual friendship. Two or more people of good will share in a familiar way their good desires, experiences, intuitions and thanks, seeking in the exchange support and encouragement for their spiritual or apostolic lives.

It is impossible not to suppose that from the outset of the cenobitic life there were different ways of spiritual conversation: monks sharing spiritual experiences, enriching each other with what each had received from the Spirit, expressing the centrality of Christ in their community lives. No doubt they also used it to deliberate together about questions of their life in common, so that those tasked with taking decisions could measure the feeling in the Lord present in the community. That is, to pour into the common channel, enriching it and broadening it, and in this way to deepen their following of the Lord.

We can say that wherever Christians have together sought to create fraternity, share the gifts of the Spirit or allow themselves to be guided by him, adjusting to the will of God, there has been some kind of spiritual conversation.

We will share some examples of spiritual conversation from our Jesuit tradition because it is the one we are most familiar with, while being very aware that similar experiences are found in other spiritualities. Ignatius of Loyola was a great conversationalist.[29] From the time of his convales

---

26 Book 9, ch. 10 of the *Confessions*, quoted by M. Nepper, 'Conversation spirituelle', in *Dictionnaire de spiritualité, ascetique et mystique* (Paris: Beauchesne, 1953), t. II/2, pp. 2212–2218.

27 Recorded by St Gregory the Great, *Dialogues*, bk 2, ch. 33, quoted by Nepper, 'Conversation spirituelle'.

28 Nepper, 'Conversation spirituelle'.

29 **Translator's note**: St Ignatius, the founder and inspiration of what would become the Society of Jesus, was a sixteenth-century minor Spanish nobleman from the Basque town of Loyola. Severely wounded in battle against the French at Pamplona, he retreated to the family castle for a lengthy convalescence, where, bored and bed-bound, he read the lives of the saints and felt a call to serve God. Once recovered, he set out as a simple pilgrim to learn what God wanted of him.

cence in his family home in Loyola, following his conversion, he began to speak of spiritual matters with those close to him, 'and the whole time he spoke with those in the house he used to spend on things of God, with which he did their souls good.'[30] Subsequently, while staying in Manresa between March 1522 and February 1523, he relished his encounters with spiritual people. 'At this time he still used to talk sometimes with spiritual people, who thought he was genuine and wanted to talk to him because, although he had no knowledge of spiritual things, still in his speaking he showed much fervour and a great will to go forward in the service of God.'[31] But at this point he made a U-turn in the logic of his communication. As well as his own benefit, he actively sought the benefit of others: to help them by means of conversation. In Manresa 'once he began to be consoled by God and saw the fruit he was bringing forth in souls as he dealt with them, he left aside those eccentricities he had from before.'[32] Spiritual conversation will in the following years continue to be present in Ignatius's life.

One could say that the Society of Jesus was born of the spiritual conversations Ignatius held with a group of fellow students with whom he shared rooms in Paris from 1528. His 'Autobiography' recalls how three fellow students (Ignatius, Francis Xavier and Pierre Favre) not only lived together but also 'conversed'. Ignatius finally won both for Christ by means of the Spiritual Exercises.[33] Other fellow students were added to this group, attracted by spiritual conversation and the Exercises.

In 1534 the group of seven companions took the first major step after having done the Exercises, in order to give expression to a shared desire that had arisen in them. After deliberating on the form and manner, they decided to strengthen their unity with a private vow in the chapel of Montmartre on 15 August that year.

Spiritual conversations appear in the list of ministries of the first Jesuits. Ignatius's collaborator Jerónimo Nadal would claim that the Society of Je-

---

30 Ignatius of Loyola, 'Reminiscences (Autobiography)', in *Personal Writings*, translated with introductions and notes by Joseph A. Munitiz and P. Endean (London: Penguin, 1996), 11.
31 Ignatius of Loyola, 'Autobiography', 21.
32 Ignatius of Loyola, 'Autobiography', 29
33 Ignatius of Loyola, 'Autobiography', 82. **Translator's note**: Ignatius's Spiritual Exercises, a series of contemplations and meditations that form the basis of a month-long retreat, were given orally, but later, around 1550, were set down in writing.

sus was shaped by that apostolate. In Ignatius's correspondence the words *converse* or *conversation* appear 316 times.[34]

A final type of spiritual conversation in the history of the first Jesuits is the deliberation by Ignatius and the first companions in 1539. The deliberation was aimed at taking decisions together that would lead to the foundation of a new religious order. This way of deciding together would acquire a paradigmatic value as a model of communal discernment, and we will present it later in some detail.

---

34 G. Arana, 'La conversación espiritual, instrumento apostólico privilegiado de la Compañía', *Revista de Espiritualidad Ignaciana*, 108 (2005), pp. 1–32.

Moment Two:
At the Service of Synodality

In his homily on Pentecost Sunday 2023, Pope Francis said that

> the Synod now taking place is – and should be – *a journey in accordance with the Spirit*, not a parliament for claiming rights and needs in accordance with the agenda of the world, nor an occasion for going wherever the wind blows, but the opportunity to be docile to the breath of the Spirit. For on the sea of history, the Church sets sail only with the Spirit, for he is 'the soul of the Church' ... the heart of synodality, the driving force of evangelisation. Without him, the Church is lifeless; faith is just doctrine, morality merely duty, pastoral work only toil ... Let us put the Holy Spirit back at the centre of the Church, for otherwise our hearts will not be inflamed with love for Jesus, but for ourselves. Let us put the Spirit at the beginning and the centre of the synod projects. For it is he above all whom the Church needs today! Let us say to him each day: 'Come!' And let us journey together because, just as at Pentecost, the Holy Spirit loves to descend when 'all are gathered together' (cf. Acts 2:1). Yes, to manifest himself to the world, he chose the time and place where *all were gathered together* ... That is how harmony in the Church is renewed: by journeying together with the Spirit at the centre.

Brothers and sisters, let us build harmony in the Church!'[35]

In this Church that has set out on the synodal journey, it will always be necessary to know how to dialogue, discuss, debate and argue a wide range of themes, choices and challenges, as is right in a living and dynamic body such as the Church. According to the context and circumstances none of these means of treating issues is irrelevant. But conversation is the instrument that has been most favoured for enabling a participation that – as fruit of listening to the Spirit – strengthens communion and mission. As the handbook notes, 'in a synodal style we make decisions through discernment of what the Holy Spirit is saying through our whole community.'[36]

For all Christians this is a challenge as complex as it is beautiful. To help us move in that direction the General Secretariat of the Synod has chosen conversation in the Spirit as the most appropriate method for encouraging the synod process across all the Churches in the world.[37] It is a tool that stands out for its simplicity, and, at the same time, for its depth; it allows us with great ease to hear the action of the Spirit in a group of people. It really is a providential gift.

Conversation in the Spirit has become a very effective tool for strengthening the Church, our great common channel into which we all pour, and which shapes and enriches us in the service of the whole of humanity with whom we walk. Spiritual conversation strengthens the spirituality of walking together, because listening forms us from within, as human persons and as Christians. Referring to spiritual conversation, the handbook describes it as promoting 'active participation, attentive listening, reflective speaking and spiritual discernment.'[38]

As has been noted already, in spiritual conversation it is not about each member or participant bringing his ideas, theories, interests or proposals – whether those of an individual or a group – for the group or communi-

35 Pope Francis, 'Homily of His Holiness Pope Francis on the Solemnity of Pentecost', multimedia, 28 May, 2023, www.vatican.va/content/francesco/en/homilies/2023/documents/20230528-omelia-pentecoste.html

36 *Vademecum*, p. 28.

37 **Translator's note**: 'Churches' here refers to the local or particular Churches that together make up the universal Catholic Church rather than other Christian denominations.

38 *Vademecum*, Appendix B, n. 8.

ty to adopt. Nor is it about establishing alliances and strategies to create majorities, nor the exercise of oratorical skills, nor the power of persuasion to pursue pre-designed agendas.

The aim of conversation in the Spirit is for each person to listen to the Spirit in prayer and to share their interior motions, that is, what they have felt as coming from the Lord, and pouring this into the common channel to generate communion. So this is a conversation that calls for humility, for depth and for care, with the particular characteristic, as already mentioned, of openness to the presence of the Spirit.

Based on what we have noted up to this point, we can distinguish three types of spiritual conversation:[39]

(a) that which simply aims to speak in a familiar way of the things of God;

(b) that which we can call apostolic;

(c) deliberation in common.

a) that which simply aims to speak in a familiar way of the things of God can be carried out with one or with many people. It is the conversation of what is known as spiritual friendship. It is not seeking to preach, or even less, to indoctrinate.

As to how it works, it's simply a question of each person sharing with others, in a simple and spontaneous way, what the Spirit is doing in them or how the Spirit is leading them: in their prayer, or family, or community, at work, in the mission.

'Out of the abundance of the heart, the heart speaks', as the saying goes. The interior motions of a person who freely shares his feelings in the Lord arouse different thoughts, feelings and motions in the ones who listen to him. So this method of spiritual conversation

39 There is a fourth kind of spiritual conversation, which we have not developed in the present text, namely that of spiritual direction or accompaniment. This too is concerned with spiritual motions, but in a more structured relationship. As in the other types, the aim is for the Spirit to act and for the person to allow himself to be guided by the Spirit in his or her life. The spiritual director should not introduce his or her own ideas, proposals etc. but 'remaining in the centre like the pointer of a balance, should leave the Creator to deal with the creature, and the creature with the Creator and Lord'. Quotations from the *Spiritual Exercises* will be taken from Michael Ivans SJ, *Understanding the Spiritual Exercises: Text and Commentary* (Leominster: Gracewing, 1998), here at 15.

enriches all the participants through the grace each receives. It is of great help to grow together as friends, as family or as a community of faith, and to create or strengthen fraternity with Christ at the centre. When he refers to this kind of spiritual conversation, St Ignatius speaks of conversation for mutual edification.

This kind of conversation is important in the synodal journey; those wishing to please the Lord need to support each other to make progress. We need it to grow personally and to grow as a Church by the Spirit. In her *Life*, St Teresa of Ávila writes that

> it is a great evil for a soul to be alone in the midst of such great dangers ... For this reason, I would advise those who give themselves to prayer, particularly at first, to form friendships; and converse familiarly with others who are doing the same thing. It is a matter of the greatest importance, even if it only to help each other in prayer: how much more are the many greater gains! ... Of myself I may say that, if our Lord had not revealed to me this truth, and given me the opportunity of speaking very frequently to persons given to prayer, I should have gone on falling and getting up again till I tumbled into hell. I had many friends to help me to fall; but as to getting up again, I was so much left to myself, that I wonder now I was not always on the ground. I praise God for his mercy; for it was he alone who stretched out his hand to me.[40]

b) That kind of spiritual conversation we can call apostolic is apostolic in as much as it constitutes a form of apostolate. It seeks to create a common channel, so that others can come and pour into it. We saw earlier that St Ignatius of Loyola exercised this and urged the Jesuits to do the same. Indeed, for Ignatius and his companions it was a privileged way of carrying out the apostolate, stirring in those they engaged in conversation a restless desire to give themselves in service of the kingdom. In St Teresa of Ávila we find the same, when she urges her nuns:

40 St Teresa of Ávila, *Life of St Teresa of Jesus*, ch. 8, pp. 32, 33, 37.

I ask you, for the love of God, always to order your conversation to the good of those with whom you speak, for your prayer must be for the profit of souls ... Those who, like nuns, are obliged to speak only of God act very wrongly if they dissemble in this way, except when for the purpose of doing greater good. Your language and conversation must be like this: let any who wish to talk to you learn your language; and, if they will not, be careful never to learn theirs: it may lead you to hell ... You will gain by this, because only those who understand your language will come to see you.[41]

c) The third kind of spiritual conversation takes place in a group deliberation. This is a spiritual conversation directed to a discernment in common: when, inspired by the Spirit, we seek together the common good of all. Within this kind of spiritual conversation we can find at least two formats:

1) When a community must make a particular concrete decision, for example, to open or not a new apostolic work, or close an existing one because some think it no longer fulfils the purpose for which it was created. Examples of this in religious or parish communities, institutes and so on are not lacking: at some point in their journey, they have had to deliberate together and take a concrete decision that affected a community or a work etc.

2) On other occasions it is more about seeking guidance about a way forward or discerning the situation in which a particular group finds itself. This is a much broader search than the previous: for example, a group or community may wonder about its priorities or apostolic needs in the coming years.

This type of deliberative conversation can be found often in religious life but also in the life of lay movements, parishes, dioceses, bishops' conferences and so on. Each of these institutions, according to their own constitution and structure, has different ways of making the final decision; each has a different way of living the service of authority. But in each case what is key is the active and vulnerable listening to what each person is

41 St Teresa of Ávila, *Way of Perfection*, ch. 20, 3, 4, 5.

offering in pursuit of the common good.

The kind of spiritual conversation that 'speaks in a familiar way of the ways of God' is described by José García de Castro as 'open spiritual conversation', because it is direct and spontaneous in the sense that it does not call for great preparation. García de Castro distinguishes this from spiritual conversation that he calls 'structured' or 'guided', because it follows an order and method that are accepted by those taking part in it.[42] The latter format is more directly geared to discernment and is the process recommended in the synod process: it aims to deepen a particular concrete point of the spiritual life or to be a tool for helping a group discern a decision.

These two kinds of spiritual conversation, 'open' and 'structured/guided', are of most interest to us as facilitating synodal communion. In as much as it is spontaneous and natural for believers to use, the open format comes about spontaneously and creates friendship and community. The structured/guided format called for by the synod process adds the element of discernment in common. This structured spiritual conversation is easily adapted and is already being put into practice in many parts of the Church. It is recommended as the 'synodal working method' in the *Final Document*,[43] which was endorsed by Pope Francis as an 'authoritative orientation for the Church's life and mission'.[44]

In the ecclesial context, we can describe the development of this 'synodal spiritual conversation', in which a group of people gathers in a climate of prayer, each to share the fruit of their prayer, and each to seek to listen to the Spirit both in prayer and through the contributions of the others. This conversation will always help to transcend and give depth to a meeting, whether personal or in a group. However, the 'structured synodal spiritual conversation' always takes place in a group or community, and as we shall see, requires a series of elements in order to be properly 'structured'. It is the format that helps us to strengthen communion and

42 J. García-Castro, *La voz de tu saludo: acompañar, conversar, discernir* (Santander: Sal Terrae, 2018), ch. 8.

43 *Final Document*, 105.

44 Pope Francis, 'Note of the Holy Father Francis to Accompany the Final Document of the 16th Ordinary General Assembly of the Synod of Bishops', bulletin, 25 November 2024, https://press.vatican.va/content/salastampa/en/bollettino/pubblico/2024/11/25/241125k.html

to guide us in decision-making through the discernment of God's will in specific questions.

Both kinds, but more specifically the structured/guided, are at the service of the synod's purpose: to seek from the proposals that the Spirit places in every heart to deepen communion within the Church, enabling participation of all the baptised through their specific gifts and charisms, and to enhance the mission, that it be carried out in a more Gospel-centred way. The exercise of spiritual conversation is of great value for the spiritual growth of those who take part in it and, therefore, of ecclesial communion. In both cases the protagonist is the Holy Spirit who moves in the interior of each person and communicates to him or her.

Although it belongs to the origins of the Society of Jesus, this format of spiritual conversation was forgotten until the final quarter of the twentieth century.[45] The origin of the 'oriented or guided' format as we know it today is to be found in the ISECP Group (Ignatian Spiritual Exercises for the Corporate Person), founded in Canada in 1977, which has developed and spread it.[46] ISECP has responded creatively to the needs of its time by enriching the practice of the Ignatian Exercises, considering each group as if it were a single person, animated by the Spirit and called to take decisions in common. Some years later, in Belgium, another group of Jesuits created ESDAC (*Exercices Spirituels pour un Discernement Apostolique en Commun* – 'Spiritual Exercises for Apostolic Discernment in Common').[47] ESDAC has developed methods of spiritual conversation geared

---

45 The article dedicated to spiritual conversation by M. Nepper, 'Conversation spirituelle', makes no mention of this guided spiritual conversation, nor does he relate it to the deliberation of the first Jesuits. He does not deal with spiritual conversation geared to discernment. The doctoral thesis of Darío Restrepo SJ, *Diálogo: Comunión en el Espíritu. La conversación espiritual según S. Ignacio de Loyola 1521–1556* (Bogotá: CIRE, 1975) studies the evolution of spiritual conversation from the deliberations of the first companions up to a spiritual conversation geared to discernment (e.g., p. 263), but he develops no method or guidance for such a conversation.

46 See James Borbely, *Ignatian Spiritual Exercises for the Corporate Person: Structured Resources for Group Development*, 2nd ed. (Scranton, PA: ISECP, 1989).

47 See http://esdac.net. Also Michel Bacq & ESDAC team, Brian Grogan SJ (ed.), *Communal Discernment: A Lamp for Our Synodal Path* (Dublin: Messenger, 2024), with a preface by Arturo Sosa SJ.

to apostolic discernment in continuity with those of ISECP.[48]

This means of practising spiritual conversation – guided, and geared to discernment – has its roots in the deliberations of the first Jesuits. It is an experience worth pausing to dwell on. Its methodology can inspire us in our different contexts – parishes, dioceses, ecclesial movements – as well as within religious life, wherever discernment in common is needed.

---

48 Cf. F. Nanin, 'Discernir juntos en grupos pequeños', *Manresa*, 94 (2022), pp. 61–70. The Society of Jesus's General Congregation 36, which took place in 2016, emphatically recovered the importance of spiritual conversation in the life of the Society. Decree 1, 'Companions in a mission of reconciliation and justice', highlights spiritual conversation as an essential tool for encouraging discernment in common. It defines it as 'an exchange marked by active and receptive listening and a desire to speak of that which touches us most deeply. It tries to take account of spiritual movements, individual and communal, with the objective of choosing the path of consolation that fortifies our faith, hope and love.' Documents of General Congregation 36 of the Society of Jesus, Decree 1, n. 12, at https://jesuits.eu/images/docs/GC_36_Documents.pdf

Moment Three:
The Deliberation of the First Jesuits in 1539

When the time came, Ignatius and his first companions had to sit down to converse, discern and together decide on the path ahead to follow. It was Lent 1539, and they were by now in Rome. There they made key decisions about the foundation of the new order and its form of life. We have a record of what took place at this deliberation, in the form of a kind of minutes of the meeting, which can inspire us in how to carry out a guided conversation geared to a discernment in common.[49]

As we have already noted, this is not the first time that the early Jesuits deliberated together in order to take decisions. In 1534 they had decided to take vows of poverty and chastity, as well as a vow to go to Jerusalem. Once there, they would decide whether to stay or return. They had given themselves a year to await a boat to the Holy Land, but none was available. Unable to go, they pursued the alternative path they had agreed on, to offer themselves to the pope, for him to send them where they were most needed. The group was conscious of being a community gathered by the Lord, but the time had come for the pope to disperse them. And so,

---

49 *Monumenta Ignaciana*, series Tertia, I, 1–7, translated into English by Dominic Maruca SJ and available at the Portal to Jesuit Studies at Boston College as 'The Deliberations of Our First Fathers (1539)', https://jesuitportal.bc.edu/research/documents/. All the quotes, unless otherwise indicated, are from this short document. In both this chapter and throughout our book we are greatly indebted to some typewritten pages by José Antonio García Rodríguez on discernment in common which remain unpublished. Many of the ideas there are collected in an interview with him by C. Jiménez, 'El discernimiento apostólico en común. Entrevista a José Antonio García', *Manresa*, 90 (2018), pp. 27–37.

> We decided to assemble before the day of separation and discuss for a number of days our common calling and the style of life we had adopted ... Our views and opinions were highly varied. We were in perfect accord in single-ness of purpose and intent: namely, to discover the gracious design of God's will within the scope of our vocation. But when it came to the question of which means would be more efficacious and more fruitful, both for ourselves and for our neighbour, there was a plurality of views.

They had a single purpose, a common good that all were pursuing, 'to discover the gracious design of God's will'. But in respect of the means, there was a 'plurality of views'. Knowing that God never denies his grace to those who seek it with a humble and simple heart, together they decided beforehand to put at the basis of their discernment some spiritual measures and right intention:

> Finally, we decided and resolved unanimously to devote ourselves to prayer, the celebration of the Holy Sacrifice and meditation, in a manner even more fervent than usual; and after we had diligently expended all human effort, we would then cast all our cares upon the Lord, trusting in him who is so good and generous. He imparts his good spirit to every-one who petitions him in humility and simplicity of heart; in fact, he is incredibly lavish in his gifts to everyone, never does he disappoint anyone. We were confident that he would in no way fail us, but since his kindness is without measure, he would assist us beyond our fondest hopes and expectations.

Together with these spiritual measures, the first Jesuits also exercised 'our human energies' to consider questions 'worthy of careful consideration and prolonged inquiry':

> Our procedure was this: all day long we reflected and med-itated on the subject; prayer was also enlisted as a source

of light. At night each person proposed to the group what he considered the better and more expedient course. In this way we hoped that all of us could embrace as the truer judgement the view that was recommended by the force of stronger arguments and enjoyed a majority of votes.

In their deliberation their aim was that 'absolutely no course of action adopted by us would be the fruit merely of our own personal ingenuity and reasoning. Rather, we simply assented to whatever the Lord inspired and the Apostolic See subsequently confirmed and approved.' What was to be brought to the conversation was uniquely what the Lord had inspired and welcomed in an ecclesial spirit. This activity requires discernment.

In this initial description of the deliberations that would give rise to the new institute, it is possible to glimpse some of the basic elements of the method they employed. Spiritual discernment in common requires, as a starting point, a renewed and conscious option for God-Love as the foundation. It calls for a very specific spiritual environment, expressed in prayer and the Eucharist, as well as the use of human energies. Finally, it involves two alternative times of seeking: personally and as a group. The personal involves different kinds of activity: reflection, meditation, prayer and Examen (review). The group activity, meanwhile, has four phases: sharing of personal views, examination of different points of view, recognition of what is 'the truer judgement', and, finally, the shared decision, whether by majority consensus or unanimity.

Spiritual discernment in common presupposes that God has a clear will, a concrete dream, for each member as well as each group or community. This is difficult for sceptical modern men and women to accept. But if we do not believe that God has a specific will and a loving plan for us, there can be neither discernment nor the spiritual conversation that enables it.

The seeking of this will, of this dream, has to be carried out from God's Spirit and not from the individual spirit of each of us; neither can it be from ideology or psychological compulsion. This implies an open listening, an attentiveness to the spiritual perception of others in a vulnerable way, that is, openness to being changed, allowing oneself to be taken over and affected, recognising that the Spirit also speaks through others. What God wants of us also reaches us through a deep listening of what the Spirit is saying to each of us, not only to the strongest. In this process, the strong make themselves weak, and the weak find their strength. Conversation has placed us on an equal footing. Excluded from this are the corridor whispers, the pressure groups and other more or less covert ways of influencing 'public opinion'. Each one brings to the table the fruit of his or her meditation and prayer.

But this sharing of how the Spirit was moving each person in relation to the question being discerned did not also prevent them expressing their fears, uncertainties, aspirations, desires and hopes. Nor did it prevent them telling each other what they had detected in what they had heard of pride or desire for power or security, which sometimes appeared in the inclinations of some of them. It was essential for the companions that this deliberative process should not break the unity of heart and minds.[50] They were engaged in building a common channel. This was an essential element that the normal way of discussing did not per se guarantee, and even less today, with the ideological disagreements that exist.

The process was supposed to be effective, to enable them to reach a decision. Until that point the group decisions, fruit of their discernment in common, were made by voting. However, the decisions arising from the 1539 'Deliberations' – without doubt the most important of all, in creating the institute and agreeing to obey the authority of one of them – were adopted unanimously.

In present-day processes of deliberation in common, the decision is taken either by voting or by coming to a group consensus, or by the one who has the gift of authority. Which it will be depends on the kind of topic or decision being discerned, as well as on the kind of group or community that is doing the discernment. But in every case, the decision is made after listening to what each person has felt in the Lord.

---

50 **Translator's note**: the *unio animorum* – *unión de ánimos* in Spanish – is a phrase used by Ignatius in the *Constitutions* to refer to the maintaining of communion between Jesuits who might be dispersed across the world and seldom see each other. It is translated into English as 'unity of hearts and minds', although *ánimo* has the connotation of spirit and soul: this is not a meeting of minds in the sense of agreeing but more a spiritual union born of shared purpose and a common way of doing things.

The method followed

Ignatius of Loyola is not recognised in the history of spirituality for any great originality of content in his *Spiritual Exercises* or the *Constitutions* of the Society of Jesus. Both owe a great deal to the existing spiritualities on which they drew. The great contribution Ignatius is known for is his proposed method for helping people, through the Exercises and its discernment rules, whose content can be found in the literature of the desert fathers and other texts he read. In this case of deliberation, the help he offers comes also in the method he developed. Spiritually conversing and deliberating together under the guidance of the Spirit has its rules and, as we shall see, the first Jesuits made them explicit. In the 'Deliberations' of 1539 there are three key steps that can shed light on our own synodal deliberations: 1) define the question to be decided; 2) pay attention to interior dispositions; and 3) a way of communicating with each other that avoids confrontation. All this, of course, in a climate of prayer.

Define well the matter for discernment

The first Jesuits managed this in their deliberations. They saw that the pope was beginning to disperse them, each according to his vocation, and that, without a commitment to unity among them, they would squander what God had done with them. So they defined clearly what they had to decide: whether or not to have a service of unity that would help them remain together as a body.

In these kinds of processes, the topic to be discerned must be clear to all those taking part. In this deliberation the early Jesuits did not discern ends; that is, they did not ask whether they wished to be better, or whether they had to improve their service of the Lord or to carry out his will. Rather, they sought the means that would best lead to that end.

The first topic that they dealt with was whether, after being dispersed by the pope (who wanted to send them to different parts of Europe), the rest should continue to be concerned for them and keep each other informed of their doings, or whether they were to care only for others, outside the Society. They agreed to remain bound to each other. That first decision having been made, another doubt then arose: whether they should take a vow of obedience to one among them, and whether – which was the same

41

thing – they should create a new religious order to keep them united even after being dispersed by the pope.

This decision was harder for them. 'We devoted many days to personal prayer and reflection in seeking a solution to this question, but could find none which set our minds at peace.' After considering various ways to resolve the impasse, including 'withdrawing to some secluded place and remain there for thirty or forty days', they opted to remain in Rome, devoting the mornings to prayer and the afternoons to their apostolates. They also saw the need of proposing some interior attitudes in order better to be led by the Spirit.

Attending to interior dispositions

As we saw earlier, a prayerful atmosphere would be essential. Some questions, because of their importance, need more time in prayer. The *Spiritual Exercises* were always involved in these deliberations: its times for making of an election, its rules for discernment, as well as a number of general principles that appear there either explicitly or implicitly. One of Ignatius's pieces of guidance seems especially apt for spiritual conversation. At the start of the *Exercises*, a 'presupposition' is proposed as a way of easing the communication between the one who is giving and the one who is making the retreat (the exercitant):

> So that the giver of the Exercises and the exercitant may the better help and benefit each other, it must be presupposed that every good Christian should be readier to justify than to condemn a neighbour's statement. If no justification can be found, one should ask the other in what sense the statement is to be taken, and if that sense is wrong the other should be corrected with love. Should this not be sufficient, let every appropriate means be sought whereby to have the statement interpreted in a good sense and so to justify it.[51]

This presupposition to every conversation without doubt creates a ready predisposition to listen to and take on board what each brings to

51 *Spiritual Exercises*, 22.

the table, seeking always to interpret in a charitable way what is heard. It is safe to presume that each of those taking part in this discernment had firmly internalised this.

Faced with the difficulty of the topic to be decided, they needed to seek fresh assistance, allowing them to go deeper into the attitudes called for by spiritual conversation geared to discernment. 'For each and every one', three steps were prescribed:

The first step was *to ask God for the opposite of what each in fact inclined to*: 'each should so dispose himself, so devote himself to prayer, the Holy Sacrifice, and meditation, that he make every effort to find peace and joy in the Holy Spirit concerning the vow of obedience. Each must strive, insofar as it depends on his personal efforts, so to dispose himself that he would rather obey than command, whenever glory to God and praise to his Majesty would follow in equal measure.'

In this way they tried to come to the conversation with the greatest inner flexibility in order to be more easily moved by the Spirit – emptying themselves of their *a priori*, as we would say now, letting go of possible affective or ideological ties. In seeking an interior acceptance of what seemed to them at the outset most difficult or desirable took them out of their comfort zone. In the *Exercises*, when one feels very tied to one particular choice prior to entering into discernment, St Ignatius makes this suggestion:

> It is to be noted that when we experience either an attachment or a repugnance, which are against actual poverty, when we are not indifferent towards poverty or riches, a great help towards extinguishing such a disordered attachment is to ask in the colloquies (even though it goes against carnal instinct) that Our Lord should choose us for actual poverty. And to desire, beg, and plead for this, provided it be for the service and praise of his Divine Majesty.[52]

The second step was *to assume their own freedom and responsibility before God to the very end* 'that no one of our band should talk over this

52 *Spiritual Exercises*, 157.

matter with another or ask his arguments. In this way, no one would be swayed by another's reasoning or disposed more favourably towards embracing obedience rather than towards rejecting it, or vice versa. Our aim was for each to consider as more desirable what he had derived from his personal prayer and meditation.' Cutting off communication between them is what nowadays we would see as a way of avoiding lobbies and public opinion pressure groups, in order to welcome more readily what comes from above.

The third step was *to consider from a distance what is best, in an independent manner, and to be prepared to take ownership of the decision reached by the group.* 'Each should consider himself unrelated to our congregation, into which he never expected to be received. With such a disposition, no emotional involvement would sway his judgement more one way or the another; rather, as an extern, he might freely advance for discussion his opinion concerning the taking or rejecting of obedience, and thus he could judge and approve that course of action which he believes will promote God's greater service and most securely assure our Society's permanence.' Imagining themselves an outsider to the congregation, they were able to take a healthy distance from the issue, in such a way that they sought the common good rather than their own good, and in this way could ponder what was best.

The double round: all seek the common good without confrontation
Inwardly disposed in the ways mentioned above, on one day they set out their views and reasons against obedience: 'With these dispositions of mind and heart as a preparation, we were to assemble on the following day. We agreed that each in turn should propose all disadvantages whatsoever against obedience and all the counterarguments which he had derived from his private reflection, meditation and prayer.'

The next day they all took the opposite position: 'Then on the following day our discussion centred on the contrary view, advancing for consideration all the advantages and benefits of the vow of obedience that each had drawn from his prayerful reflection. Thus each in his turn proposed the conclusions at which he had arrived.'

This is what we mean by *the double round*: one day all are in favour and inwardly disposed to it, and the next day they all take the opposite stance. The double round should not be confused with the three phases or rounds of conversation in the Spirit that we will look at later. The double round is very important for 'not breaking the unity of hearts'. Nobody is at any point opposed to anyone else; they are always on the same side. So there are never rivals, only companions seeking together the will of God, ready to welcome it, whatever it be. No one is constrained, but the dialectic of confrontation is avoided. Instead of arguing, we converse, each pouring into the common channel.

What is brought to the conversation are the inner feelings or reasons that have been encountered during prayer. Each one, in turn, pours out what he or she has drawn from their prayer and meditation. When the double round has been taken, for and against the matter submitted for deliberation, each one stays to internalise, also in a climate of prayer, his own movements and those of others, such that the group comes peacefully to a view:

> For many days we discussed the various aspects of this question, analysing and weighing the relative merits and cogency of each argument, always allowing time for our customary practices of prayer, meditation and reflection. Finally, with the help of God, we came to a decision. We concluded, not only by a majority vote but indeed without a single dissenting voice, that it would be more advantageous and even essential for us to vow obedience to one of our number in order to attain three aims: first, that we might better and more exactly pursue our supreme goal of fulfilling the divine will in all things; second, that the Society might be more securely preserved; and finally, that proper provision might be made for those individual matters, of both spiritual and temporal moment, that will arise.

They continued in this way for three months, deciding on the specifics of the new form of life. The method, as can be seen here, is for matters of importance and all involved should participate: the issue being discussed affects everyone in the process. For those not on the inside, there are no inner movements to share.

One advantage of this method is that after open and vulnerable listening, the journey undertaken with others allows everyone to better understand the reasons for the decision. This is the case even when the final decision differs from what one felt before the process, or even from what one hoped for during the process. This way of walking together brings about communion.

Moment Four:
A Way of Sharing and Listening That Opens Us to the Spirit

Synodal spiritual conversation has its rules. Some of these are the same as those that operate in conversations than enrich civic life, which we considered earlier. But what really helps bring the light we need is a way of listening and speaking that helps us to open ourselves up to the action of the Spirit in the Church and in our lives.

When a structured spiritual conversation is geared to decision-making, it does not need to deal explicitly with spiritual or religious themes and content. But it does involve a *discernment in common*.[53] This process calls for a way of speaking and listening that flows from listening to the Spirit of the Lord, who creates communion and Church. This kind of spiritual conversation asks us to attune our listening, so that we pay attention to the spiritual motions that are taking place in others, as well those taking place in the whole group or community. An attitude of welcome and reverence towards others springs from within us, one that takes seriously the fact that everyone is trying to make space for a Word that comes from above, from the Spirit, by means of the inner self of each participant. Spiritual conversation calls for an atmosphere of trust and loyalty so that everyone can express themselves freely and openly.

---

53 **Translator's Note**: 'discernment in common' is distinct from ordinary discernment in that the discerning subject is a group or community rather than an individual person. The process is also referred to as 'communal discernment' or 'communal apostolic discernment'.

What is of value in conversation in the Spirit is not so much unanimity of opinion or even a shared point of view but the communion of hearts in the search for a common good and the desire to obey God's will, whatever that be. Having different perspectives enriches the search and discernment in common. It helps to discover the different ways in which the Spirit is present and at work in the group. Two basic skills or practices make up spiritual conversation: active listening and intentional speaking.[54]

Active and vulnerable listening

Active listening accepts and listens to everyone as they are and in what they say. We call it active listening because in listening attention is paid at many levels to the participation of others. It is about listening with empathy, always trying to understand and take in what others are saying or want to say, and what they have experienced internally, which they often express awkwardly. Therefore listening must be kindly, always seeking to interpret in a good sense what the other is saying. At its root is trusting that the Spirit is or can be at work in everyone and may be speaking to us through them. A radical acceptance of the other person ends up being part of the spiritual conversation.

When we listen, we *just listen*. Rather than preparing what we are going to say, we focus all our attention on the other person and on what they are saying. Nor do we allow our ideological filters or our prejudices to sift what we hear, but try instead to make room for the other. We do not judge the one who speaks nor what they say. We simply let her be herself, allowing her to express herself freely from within. Listening in this way is an act of deep respect and love. It is a listening that avoids commenting on what we hear, avoids even giving approval or encouragement, so as not to influence the interventions of the other group members, allowing them to be as free as possible. When it is not your turn to speak, active listening is your main task.

Active listening does not leave us as we are: it affects us, it moves us in-

---

54 A very practical document, with thorough pedagogical explanations of the process of spiritual conversation geared to discernment in common, and which has inspired these pages, is that of the Jesuits of Canada, *Communal Apostolic Discernment: A Toolkit*, https://bit. ly/3XMYRhV, see pp. 5–9.

wardly. We must also seek to discern these movements that are caused in us by what we hear, to see where they come from and where they lead us.

There is a kind of *armoured listening*. Sometimes in groups we already know each other very well and have certain expectations about what others are going to say. Sometimes we do this even when people are not speaking from a viewpoint opposed to our own. We think we know where another is coming from, we anticipate what he's going to say and we put up barriers. This is not how we welcome what the Spirit might be saying through this person to the community. This was how Jesus was received in his hometown. They knew he was the son of the carpenter and Mary. They knew his brothers and sisters; they knew very well who he was. It is this attitude that made Jesus exclaim, 'Prophets are not without honour except in their hometown, and among their own kin.' Mark notes that Jesus 'could do no deed of power there, except that he laid his hands on a few sick people and cured them' (Mk 6:3–5).

There is also an *ideological listening*. This is what happens when you listen to the contributions of others only in order to refute them. While the other person is speaking, you have already formulated your conclusions. You know how the conversation should end; inwardly, you prepare your intervention either to reject or neutralise the other's. The Gospel is full of examples when Jesus is asked questions to test him (e.g., Mt 22:15, 35; Mk 10:2). For those already entrenched in their ideas of who God is and should be, Jesus' response will not change them. Hence the story of the adulterous woman (Jn 8:3–11), whom the teachers of the law bring before Jesus. Their intention is not to have a frank conversation with him but to lay a trap to accuse him, because they are attached to the letter of the law. Jesus' discourses on the bread of life and the controversy this arouses among his listeners are another helpful example (cf. Jn 6:28–59).

Ideological listening too fails to develop a listening to the Spirit, who, as the Gospel of John tells us, 'blows where it chooses, and you hear the sound of it, but you do not know where it comes from or where it goes' (Jn 3:8).

Another kind of listening, *the kind that a disciple makes to his master or vice versa*, is equally not proper to a conversation geared to discernment in common, in which all are disciples in the holy school of the Spirit, all are listeners of the Word, and all contribute on an equal footing.

In structured synodal spiritual conversation geared to discernment in common it is important that the group – or at least the facilitator – be aware of potential boycotters of discernment. They may be very subtle; they may use – consciously or unconsciously – strategies for reaching pre-determined conclusions, which impede the work of the Spirit. It can help to have a moment of examination at the end of the spiritual conversation to detect these failures of discernment.

The listening called for in spiritual conversation is not only open but *vulnerable*. It is a matter of working out what we have heard from others, what has moved us inwardly, recognising how it has affected us in our inner depths and of welcoming the new grace that reaches us via others. It is a listening that is open to allowing ourselves to be changed by what we have heard, after pondering it within ourselves in prayer, and to accepting it as coming from the Spirit. This implies being open to the possibility that what the other says could change our own preconceptions, certainties, points of view, and the way we see problems.

One of the most positive spiritual effects of spiritual conversation is that it moves us out from where we were. A beautiful example of this vulnerable listening is Jesus' conversation with the Syrophoenician woman. In this encounter Jesus was surprised and amazed by the sincerity and steadfast, persevering faith of this pagan woman who asked him to make her daughter well. Even though Jesus came to save everyone, he believed that the Father's plan was not to go beyond the borders of Israel, telling the Syrophoenician woman: 'I was sent only to the lost sheep of the people of Israel.' Jesus' openness and vulnerable listening in conversation with her caused him to be moved by her faith and to work a miracle. He changed his initial response, attended to the needs of a gentile and revised his previous understanding of his mission (cf. Mt 15:21–28).

Intentional speaking[55]

In expressing and sharing what we have experienced in our prayer, our speaking is intentional. We try sincerely to express our own experience, feelings and thoughts about the topic at hand. We share what we feel in the Lord, the inner movements that we recognise as being produced by

55 Jesuits of Canada, *Toolkit*, pp. 5–9

the Spirit. Intentional speaking requires listening actively to oneself and, in some way, discerning what one has experienced. This means divesting ourselves of 'self-love, self-will and self-interest' and sharing unselfconsciously what we believe to be a gift of the Spirit for this topic of conversation and discernment.[56] Though it is detached and discerned, what one shares is what one sees and feels. That is what makes it intentional.

Our interventions need to be, as far as possible, *independent*, that is, avoiding dependence on the influence of another. It is also important not to be driven by one's own affective or ideological attachments. How the Lord communicates to us is unique and particular to us. In sharing intentionally, each takes responsibility for what he or she feels, what he or she interprets and what he or she says. There is a beautiful interplay between active listening and intentional speaking, thus understood, which can bring out the best in each one of us.

Spiritual conversation also requires a way of expressing ourselves, a way of sharing what has been received in prayer. *Spontaneity* may add spice to the communication and is pleasant. But it is too limited a modality for a guided, spiritual conversation geared to discernment in common, which requires a prior moment of prayer and of preparing what one is going to share with humility, succinctness and seriousness. Spontaneity is not the mode of conversation for arriving at important decisions.

Sharing from the head, from the *intelligence*, by an exchange of analyses and views, can be profound and visionary. But the ultimate source remains ourselves, when what we are hoping for is to receive a Word from God. Certainly intelligence, analyses and views are positive and must have their place in the synodal journey together. But they are not suitable for discerning by listening to what comes from the Spirit. Ringfencing ourselves within our own thoughts, studies, reasoning, subtle arguments and so on can be a temptation that prevents us from exposing ourselves inwardly in a group and from allowing ourselves to be disarmed by the Divine Goodness.

Expressing ourselves out of our *feelings* is also very valuable, but this too has its limits. It can end up being suffocating when it becomes a game of demands to be satisfied, when there is no shared channel and instead

56 *Spiritual Exercises*, 189.

the self is poured into the other. It can also end up in sentimentality or over-sensitivity, when feelings remain skin-deep. In this case it is like the seed that grows on stony ground, taking root with difficulty and superficiality and failing to develop.

The desirable form of communication in spiritual conversation, especially when it is geared to discernment, is *from the heart*, in the biblical sense, from the very centre of the person inhabited by the Lord. The heart is not a separate sphere but the crucible of all that passes through the human being. Communication with the Lord is from heart to heart, and it is from there that we communicate with others in spiritual conversation. A clean, naked and divested heart is the seat of 'inner feeling', of spiritual sensitivity, of what traditionally were known as 'the spiritual senses'. It is heart in this sense that integrates and brings out the best of spontaneity, affection and intelligence, as when Luke's Gospel tells how Mary 'treasured all these words and pondered them in her heart' (Lk 2:19, 51).

Pope Francis's encyclical *Dilexit Nos*, which was published to coincide with the conclusion of the Synod on Synodality in October 2024, begins with a chapter on the need to recover the significance of the heart, this 'profound core' of ourselves in a society that has in many ways lost sight of it.

> Even encountering others does not necessarily prove to be a way of encountering ourselves, inasmuch as our thought patterns are dominated by an unhealthy individualism. Many people feel safer constructing their systems of thought in the more readily controllable domain of intelligence and will. The failure to make room for the heart, as distinct from our human powers and passions viewed in isolation from one another, has resulted in a stunting of the idea of a personal centre, in which love, in the end, is the one reality that can unify all the others.[57]

It is in the heart that we discern, where we welcome what is of God and

57 Pope Francis, *Dilexit Nos* (Vatican: The Holy See, 2024), 10, https://www.vatican.va/content/francesco/en/encyclicals/documents/20241024-enciclica-dilexit-nos.html

share only what is of God. St John warns, 'Do not believe every spirit, but test the spirits to see whether they are from God' (1 Jn 4:1). Cassian, for his part, uses the image of money changers who must learn to detect pure gold from that which has not been purified in the melting-pot, weighing the coins to see whether what glitters is, in fact, gold. 'And, above all, whatever thoughts creep into our hearts, whatever maxims suggest themselves to us, let us examine them with the utmost diligence. We must consider whether they be in full consonance with the supreme norm of the Holy Spirit and can withstand the test of divine fire, or ... if they instead arise from the pedantry and pomposity of the philosophy of the age, even while outwardly they be put to us in a cloak of piety.'[58]

Benefits of conversation in the Spirit

Conversation in the Spirit encourages personal growth and helps the members of the group to know each other. It gives the opportunity to grow in a deep and personal communication that is hard to achieve without the aid of a structure and direction for the conversation, and the cultivation of inner dispositions.

It can be of great help in resolving conflicts, reconciling the estranged, overcoming polarisation in a group, building and deepening communion and, if there is a shared mission involved, in strengthening it or in finding new paths inspired by the Spirit.

In the case of conversation being geared to decision-making, when that decision is reached and taken on board by all, it unifies the community, strengthening its bonds. All those taking part will feel involved in the project that the decision leads to, which will give it unusual consistency and energy.

When it becomes habitual, conversation in the Spirit is a school of virtue. The way of listening and speaking and the inner dispositions called for gradually shape habits of the heart in those who take part: a peaceful, open listening; a spirit of participation, gratuity, humility, discretion, fraternity and obedience (which is also a virtue).

---

58 John Cassian, *Colaciones*, vol. I, I, XX, p. 30.

Moment Five:
Inner Dispositions[59]

Synodality, notes the synod's *Final Document*, 'is primarily a spiritual disposition', one that 'flows from the action of the Holy Spirit'. It requires 'listening to the Word of God, contemplation, silence and conversion of the heart' and calls for 'asceticism, humility, patience and a willingness to forgive and be forgiven'.[60] We have begun a process, assisted by spiritual conversation, that can help us grow in gospel dispositions, in deeper listening and in healing wounds and divisions.

Whether spontaneous or structured, spiritual conversation has its rules, which to some extent shape those who participate in it. At the same time it requires some prior attitudes or dispositions on the part of those taking part. The spiritual traditions of both East and West offer us some valuable advice on how to be more truly led by the Holy Spirit, showing us the path of conversion.

(a): Speaking and listening as equals
We have already said that spiritual conversation is not argument, or dispute, or debate, nor even a dialogue on spiritual matters. It is often the case that some of the participants in a synodal spiritual conversation are well trained in theology. This can cause spiritual conversation to drift into

---

59 We need to insist on the importance of prior dispositions so that spiritual conversation is truly 'in the Spirit' and that discernment, whether personal or in common, is a true search for God's will. Informative articles are those of A. Guillén, 'Los engaños del discernimiento', *Manresa*, 82 (2010), pp. 15–25, and T. Catalá & I. Boné, 'Disposiciones personales ante el discernimiento comunitario', *Manresa*, 90 (2018), pp. 49–62.

60 *Final Document*, 43.

theory, into an intellectual analysis of problems, into rational exposition and defence of ideas. Others taking part might have leadership or coordinating roles in the Church and be tempted to try to persuade others to embrace their own views in order quickly to come up with effective solutions. Here too the risk is of avoiding a listening to the Spirit and to what the Spirit is saying through each one.

This is not to cast doubt on the great importance and undoubted value of academic training, of intellectual rigour, of the ability to defend one's own ideas, of arguing and of resolving effectively certain issues. All of these have their place in the synodal path. But spiritual conversation has its own specific dynamic, in which these qualities can become an obstacle. Ideas, reasoning and argumentation can stifle the Spirit, making it hard to listen deeply to the prompts and suggestions of the Spirit that may be surfacing.

As the ancient wisdom of the Desert Fathers gathered by Cassian reminds us,

> It often happens, whether through diabolical delusion or human failing – for there is no one in this world not subject to error – that he who possesses more knowledge and greater natural insight will develop false ideas; while a slower and less far-reaching intelligence has a broader and more certain grasp of things. No one, however wise he be, can afford to believe that he can dispense with his brother's advice. Satan's illusions will lead him into deceiving himself, and he will not escape the snares of elation and pride. Who can arrogate such independence to himself without incurring irreparable harm?'[61]

God has not promised success to the strongest, the most educated or the most intelligent. In spiritual conversation, therefore, we leave hierarchies, roles and functions out of it. In spiritual conversation we are all

61   John Cassian, *Colaciones*, vol. II, XVI, XII, p. 69.

sisters and brothers, disciples in the school of the Spirit, and on an equal footing. This does not exclude us having a diversity of charisms, nor that on our journey some of us have the charism of authority, teaching, prophecy and so on. But when we converse spiritually, we divest ourselves of these in order to contribute and to receive what the Spirit is saying to each of us personally and through others. What we hear enables us better to exercise our various charisms.

(b): The subject of the conversation should always be ruled by the common good

Self-referentiality has no place here. Those who always end up talking about themselves, their exploits or their ideas, tend not to recognise the common riverbed and to depart from the topic. The subject of spiritual conversation, on the other hand, is a common good, which gives the conversation a positive tone. In a deliberative spiritual conversation, a good is being discerned. It is reasonable to highlight dangers or threats to the good being sought, but the good itself must not be lost sight of. As the Book of Sirach (Ecclesiasticus) teaches us, 'the knowledge of wickedness is not wisdom' (19:22).

There is a way of talking about the challenges and problems of the Church that is unhelpful, and this quotation from Sirach rejects it. It is a sterile way. We will not find salvation in mere knowledge of evil, in rigorously examining what is wrong in our society or in the Church, in having perfect diagnoses of the ill we are battling and using that knowledge to plan our action to combat it. This usually ends in that exaltation of our will known as voluntarism, acting as if everything depended wholly on us.

We are on the side of good; we have been saved. We do not only react against evil; we wish to propose what is good. We live out of an original gift that we seek to channel and put into practice in an ambiguous culture, so that it may be fruitful. Perfect maps of the evil against which we struggle may be helpful, but they will not make us wise. We need to be careful, too, that in engaging with evil we can be infected by it. We must focus not on evil but on the good that is revealed to us, sometimes dimly. Wisdom comes from what is good, from the gift we have received, from welcoming the Word – love that comes down from above – and embodying it in words and deeds. This will require us to grow in awareness in order to know how to see the good that is revealed to us in life, which most of the time comes to us in fledgling form.

(c): Humility in the way we share and listen

Spiritual conversation makes us humble in the sense that, at the outset, we do not think we possess the truth but are open to contributing what has been shown to us and to welcoming what is offered to us through others.

Active listening calls for humility, openness, patience and engagement. What St Paul recommends is very pertinent here: 'Do nothing from selfish ambition or conceit, but in humility regard others as better than yourselves. Let each of you look not to your own interests, but to the interests of others. Let the same mind be in you that was in Christ Jesus' (Phil 2:3–5). Spiritual conversation educates us in a reverential respect for the contributions of others. Moreover, it often leads us to change our assumptions, our ideas of others or of the subject at hand.

A temptation in spiritual conversation often pointed out by spiritual authors is that of vanity, the temptation to exaggerate the gift received. It is the temptation to elevate oneself above what one has experienced: this is vanity in speaking. With her Magnificat, Mary teaches us how to accept the graces we have humbly received. We are not responsible for them; they have been given to us. What remains is for us to be grateful.

A certain care is advisable when speaking and sharing what we receive from the Lord in spiritual conversation. St Ignatius in one of his letters referred to the danger of falling into two temptations. On the one hand it is easy, when communicating, subtly to **add to** what we have received from the Spirit. On the other hand we may, through shame, simple respect or false humility **subtract from** it, reducing the grace that has been given to us, and in this way prevent it bearing the fruit for which it was given.

Interior experience can be inexpressible, hard to translate into words. When it comes to interpreting it, in order not to add to it and thereby distort, twist or undermine the gift received, St Ignatius in one of his letters invites us to 'conform with the commandments, with the precepts of the Church and with obedience to our superiors, and full of complete humility because *the same divine Spirit is in everything*.[62] The Spirit not only speaks to us, but also to others. In order not to add to it, it is helpful to consider that what has been given to us we receive *in* the Church and *for the good of* the Church.

When it comes to subtracting the meaning of what we have been shown, St Ignatius warns that 'here one needs more care than anywhere else'. A gift might end up not bearing fruit. So the criterion here is 'to pay more attention to the needs of others than to our own desires', and the strategy is 'to proceed when trying to help others like a person crossing a ford'. If it helps others, go ahead; but if not, wait for a better moment. The gift we receive in the spiritual life is designed to bear fruit for the good of the Church and for others.

Another point worth paying attention to is the moment after we receive the grace given to us. For while the grace is from the Lord, it is quite possible that what comes after is not Spirit-led and can pervert it. Often we wrap the grace received in our speeches, habits, ideologies, subjecting it to our concepts or judgements, with the result that it ends up bearing little resemblance to what was actually shown to us. It is as if we 'round up' the grace. 'New wine should be put into fresh wineskins' (Lk 3:38). This means that we must avoid diluting the newness of the grace we have received by putting it in old containers that adulterate it. The grace received is what it is and is not to be not rounded up by adding to it or subtracting from it in order to make it fit with what we already think.

(d): Discretion is a virtue in discernment-oriented spiritual conversation
Discretion, *diakrisis*, is the capacity for discernment or spiritual prudence. Cassian relates it to the gospel text of the eye as the lamp of the body:

> This is the prudence that the Saviour calls in the Gospel the eye as the lamp of the body. 'The lamp of your body is the eye. So if your eye is healthy, your whole body will be full of light; but if your eye is diseased, your whole body will be in darkness' (Mt 6:22–23). [Prudence] discerns, in fact, all of

---

62 Ignatius of Loyola, 'Letter to Teresa Rejadell, 18 June 1536', in *Personal Writings*, p. 134. Italics added.

man's thoughts and deeds, examining them in the light to see what it is we ought to do. If this inner eye is evil, that is to say, if we are devoid of knowledge or sure judgement and allow ourselves to be deceived by error and self-sufficiency, our whole body will be in darkness. In other words, everything in us, intelligence and actions, will be as it were shrouded in the most obscure darkness, for vice is blind and passion is the mother of darkness. 'If then the light in you is darkness,' the Lord goes on to say, 'how great is the darkness!' (Mt 6:23). It is doubtless the case that, if we judge falsely and walk blindly in the night of ignorance, then so too our thoughts and deeds, which flow from these as from their source, will also be shrouded in the darkness of sin.[63]

The thoughts we have to discern are of three types; for Cassian it is important to discern their origin. 'It is important for us to know, first of all, that there are three sources from which our thoughts originate: God, the devil and ourselves.'[64]

St Ignatius in his *Exercises* tells us something similar: 'I presuppose that there are three kinds of thought processes in me, one sort that are properly mine and arise simply from freedom and will, and two other sorts that come from outside, one that comes from the good spirit and the other from the bad.'[65] Ignatius also invites us to examine the development of our thought processes:

> We must pay close attention to the whole course of our thoughts; if the beginning, middle and end are entirely good and tend towards what is wholly right, this is a sign of the good angel. But if the course of the thoughts suggested to us leads us finally to something bad or distracting, or less good than what one had previously intended to do, or if in the end the soul is weakened, upset or distressed, losing the peace, tranquillity and quiet previ-

63 Cassian, *Colaciones*, vol. I, II, II, p. 39.
64 Cassian, *Colaciones*, vol. I, XIX, p. 29.
65 *Spiritual Exercises*, 32.

ously experienced – all this is a clear sign of the bad spirit, the enemy of our progress and eternal well-being.[66]

These rules are to be applied in what we are going to share, and when discerning the resonances of what others share, during the conversation in the Spirit.

We must not allow ourselves to be distracted by the words and expressions of another age. Reality is what it is. It may be difficult for us moderns to accept these origins of our thoughts. Irenée Hausherr, a scholar of the Eastern Fathers, is well aware of the difficulty of talking about this when she writes, 'Underneath even the psychic elements of which we are unaware, there exists a force: a series of forces, rather, and fearsome at that! Modern people of course refuse to call these dark powers demons or spirits. But changing what we call them does not get rid of or essentially alter what they are. Our ancient psychoanalysts also use more neutral words, such as *logismós* or *prosbolé*.'[67]

These are thoughts and suggestions that assail us and seek to lead us from within. Some thoughts or suggestions may steer us more than others: some move us towards good, others towards evil and self-destruction. St Ignatius refers to 'the enemy of human nature' who acts at times as an 'angel of light', bringing thoughts and suggestions that appear to us good, yet which always militate against our good.[68] Discernment is about learning to be aware of and become familiar with the motions within us in order to welcome the friendly motions and reject those of the enemy. To do this, we must examine their origin and see where they lead us.

(e): Renouncing our own will

This is something to pay close attention to, for in discernment in common, and thus in spiritual conversation, self-interest or self-will often play tricks to prevent people from being 'discrete', that is, able to discern.[69]

---

66 *Spiritual Exercises*, 333.
67 Irenée Hausherr, *La direction spirituelle en Orient autrefois* (Rome: Pont. Institutum Orientalium, 1955), p. 94.
68 *Spiritual Exercises*, 7, 135.
69 **Translator's note**: like the Spanish *discreto*, 'discrete' has its origin in the Latin *discretio*, meaning the capacity to distinguish or separate things, to choose between options, that is, to discern. This is the meaning retained in the English expression 'use your discretion'.

In the Gospel there is no shortage of sayings by Jesus that today, just as then, sound harsh and difficult to accept at the outset. 'If any want to become my followers, let them deny themselves and take up their cross and follow me' (Mt 16:24). 'In the language of the Eastern ascetics (and of St Benedict), this self that must be renounced is called one's own will.'[70] Another author has interpreted this self-denial as 'cutting off one's own will and clinging to the *apsephiston*', that is, indifference to all worldly advantage, or 'how to cut off these three things: one's own will, self-justification and the desire to please'.[71]

From the start of the spiritual life, asserting one's own will and seeking one's own advantage were the first things that had to be given up in order to find God's will. This is the dynamic of losing one's life in order to gain it (Mt 16:25). And in this we must not be naïve, either personally or in our conversations, for self-will is disguised: 'one's own will, love of self, self-interest, in a word *philautía* (self-love), thanks above all to certain devout attitudes, manages to disguise itself as love of God, of which it is the implacable enemy'.[72] St Paul was no stranger to this self-assertion. 'Let each of you look not to your own interests, but to the interests of others' (Phil 2:4), he wrote, urging the Philippians to take on the 'same mind' that was in Christ Jesus (Phil 2:5). Introducing Timothy to them, Paul notes how 'all of them are seeking their own interests, not those of Jesus Christ' (Phil 2:21).

Another way of speaking of what must be given up in order to enter a spiritual conversation is of *affective and ideological attachments*. This is especially true of spiritual conversation geared to decision-making. Attachments prevent one entering into discernment. It is the pure in heart who see God. There is an extensive literature on the art of purifying the heart to become more sensitive to what the Spirit brings. The heart tends to become caught up with affections and filled with dross when those affections are disordered. A desire is driven out by a stronger desire. A passion for God and for his kingdom puts everything in its place and orders the heart. God alone is God.

---

70 Hausherr, *La direction spirituelle*, p. 161.
71 Barsanufo, letters 255 and 236, quoted by Hausherr, *La direction spirituelle*, pp. 162, 165.
72 Hausherr, *La direction spirituelle*, p, 161.

In order to discern, I must accept that I am not God and that no-thing is God. This attitude relativises all that is either not God or not given by him. Thus our attachments to things, ideas or our self-image assume their true importance and place in relation to the kingdom or God's will. If, in spite of this, a person does not succeed in freeing himself from these ties, the Ignatian suggestion for liberating the attached heart is to ask God in prayer, even if it goes against his natural desires, that the Lord may choose him for that which he rejects or which causes repugnance in him; and 'to desire, beg and plead for this, provided it be for the service and praise of his Divine Majesty'.[73]

There are meetings, which purport to be spiritual conversations, in which everyone presents their own views without having purified their own interests or their own wills. In these meetings the Spirit has not really been listened to. Once everyone has spoken and expounded, a consensus is sought in the group. Often the group is happy and feels good about the decision reached. But in reality there has been no spiritual conversation.

In Figure 1 we can assume that two subjects arrive with their view of the problem and want to take it forward. In a process of negotiation they are looking for a consensus on the basis of the points they have in common.

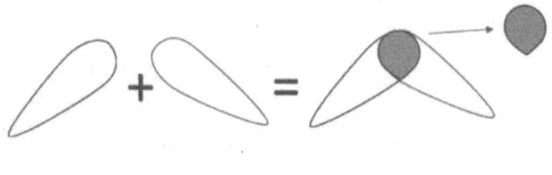

Fig. 1

What the personal interests and wills of those taking part in the conversation in the Spirit have in common is not God's will. They must lose these in order to gain in a much deeper way. When consensus is built on the basis of undiscerned self-interest, then the more diverse we are the less we have in common. The conversation lacks a common channel that is enriched and broadened by the contribution of all. The more var-

73 *Spiritual Exercises*, 157.

ied and diverse the group, the less the participants will have in common, and so the consensus reached will be that much smaller, for there will be less crossover between particular interests, as can be seen in figure 2.

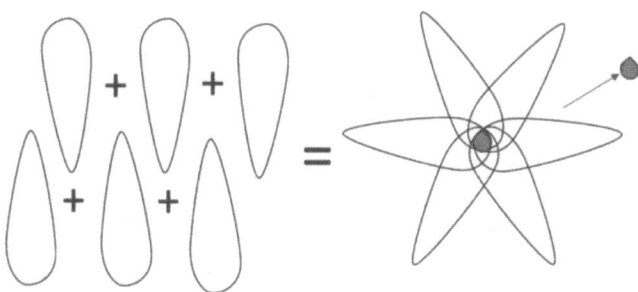

Fig. 2

That is not how we build the Church. Instead, we build Church and communion when each surrenders his or her own interests to those of Jesus Christ, and their own will in order to unite with God's will. In pouring into the common channel what has been given to us, leaving our own will or particular interests outside, we find ourselves enriched by the process.

Our common channel, the space of communion, will grow larger as we expand in number. We will be able to welcome more people, and more diverse people with more points of view, as shown in Figure 3. In this case we could speak of a consensus that has been poured forth or 'decanted'. To achieve this, we have had to step out of our own love, desire and interest, and not put the 'I' in the way of building the 'we'. From the space of communion created by spiritual conversation we can find in ourselves something that we were not aware of.

(f): Reduce the outside noise that is being internalised
In his opening address to the final session of the synod assembly in October 2024, Pope Francis spoke of the power and agency of the Holy Spirit in the life of the Church. He described the synod journey as a 'process in which the Church, submitting to the action of the Holy Spirit ... continually renews herself'. And he concluded with a hope that 'all will open

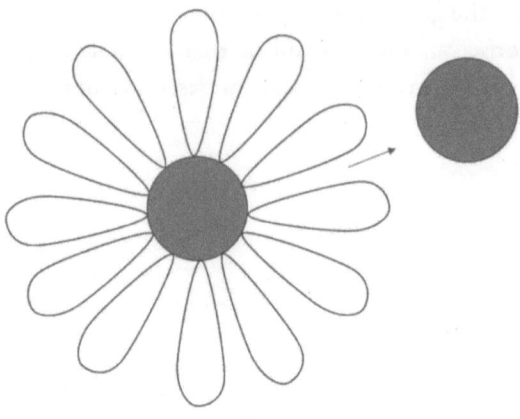

Fig. 3

themselves willingly to the action of the Holy Spirit, our trusty guide, our consolation.'[74]

When we want to receive the action of the Spirit, we often encounter interferences, and here the help of the Word of God is indispensable. Some authors have spoken of 'the dumb voices of our culture'.[75] Within us resonate the images of the films we watch, the assessments of the newspapers we read, the ideas of the discussions we listen to and so on. It would be a pity if, in our spiritual conversation, in trying to find out what the Lord wants of us and to welcome the action of the Spirit in us, we were to become mere transmitters or amplifiers of the mainstream media, today somewhat polarised in order to appeal to polarised audiences. This mainstream needs also to be neutralised in spiritual conversation and discernment. The media, usually driven by interests of various kinds, provokes a reaction within us that we have to discern and either accept or reject. For this we need to drink from deeper and cleaner waters. That means it is vital to choose where to drink from and where to nourish our spirit.

Cassian was familiar with this challenge: 'I say that it is largely up to us to correct and adjust our thoughts, and to cause holy and spiritu-

74 Pope Francis, '1st General Congregation: Opening Address', in appendix to *Final Document*, 57–60.
75 Cf. A Tornos, 'Voces mudas de la cultura entre los ejercitantes de hoy', *Manresa*, 70 (1998), pp. 129–147.

al thoughts to grow in our hearts, rather than allow earthly and carnal thoughts to prevail. That is why we regularly make use of frequent reading and meditation of Scripture, that we might procure divine thoughts for our memory.'[76]

Thoughts and suggestions will always assail us within us; we cannot avoid it. But we can avoid being internally colonised by those we do not want. Cassian compares this task of the heart to 'the grinding wheel of a millstone, which spins speedily under the effect of a swift current. Under the incessant action of the water it can neither stand still nor cease its work. However, it is up to the miller to make it grind wheat, rye or barley as he wishes. And it is true that the wheel will grind only what the one who has to do this task is pleased to introduce.'[77] In other words, it is up to us what we allow inside us: what we read, the news channels we follow, and above all, whether or not we have recourse to Scripture and other spiritual readings. For, says Cassian,

> If, as we have said, we have recourse to constant meditation on the Scriptures and evoke in our minds the recollection of supernatural realities, as well as the desire for perfection and the hope of future bliss, the thoughts which will arise therefrom cannot but be spiritual, and will keep the soul at the heights where meditation caused it to live. But if, yielding to idleness and carelessness, we should be distracted by useless or blameworthy conversation, and be overwhelmed by the cares of this world and superfluous preoccupations, then it is only logical that a kind of weed will arise that will cause to our soul a most pernicious work of grinding. And at that point the Saviour's sentence will be upon us: 'For where your treasure is, there your heart will be also' (Mt 6:21).[78]

(g): An outgoing, compassionate gaze at the world

If one of the central topics of conversation in the synodal process is the

---

76 Cassian, *Colaciones*, vol. I, I, XVII, p. 28.
77 Cassian, *Colaciones*, vol. I, I, XVII, p. 28.
78 Cassian, *Colaciones*, vol. I, I, XVII, p. 28.

Church's mission, then how it looks at the world to which it is sent is an essential spiritual disposition. The way the Trinity looks at the world in the *Exercises* is outward-focused and filled with compassion, coming out of itself in the second person to redeem the humanity for which it feels pity.[79]

This way of looking is what characterises Jesus when, on his way to relax with his disciples, 'he saw a great crowd; and he had compassion for them, because they were like sheep without a shepherd; and he began to teach them many things' (Mk 6:34). In Jesus we see this continual going out of himself, entering into and making his own the plight of those he meets. This is the inner disposition that we are to cultivate: if what happens in the world does not affect us, it is not possible to discern what God wants for it.

This outward focus means living 'on the road', walking with people on their journeys and listening to the questions that fill and trouble their hearts, making them his own. It means meeting people where they are, coming alongside them and reaching out to them 'on the often rocky roads of life'. It is to accept the pope's invitation to incarnate 'this "style" of God, who travels the paths of history and shares in the life of humanity'.[80]

There is a way of looking at the world that we cannot allow ourselves, for we no longer live in the morning of creation when God saw that 'all is good'. Nor is it Christian to look at the world in a way that demonises all that is in it, considering it evil insofar as it is marked from the beginning by sin, and therefore subject to the prince of this world. Redemption has turned the world into a *mission* for the Christian; this world, created by God and by human freedom, has been embraced by the grace and love of God, redeemed in Christ, and called to be the kingdom of God. And so, despite the world's alienation from God, the salvation of the world has, in Christ, already come about in an eschatological way, and thus shapes the Christian's mission.

Aligning ourselves with God's saving dynamic asks us not to conform ourselves to the world but to be transformed by the renewal of

---

79 *Spiritual Exercises*, 102–109.
80 Pope Francis, 'Homily at the Opening of the Synodal Path'.

our mindset, such that we may know how to discern what is God's will, what is the good that pleases him, what is perfect.[81] This way of being in the world, one that allows us to discern God's will, involves accepting God's incarnational dynamic and aligning ourselves to this dynamic of descent, attuning our inner feeling to it.[82] In short, it is a matter of accepting his cross. The triumphalism and spiritual worldliness that Francis so deplores are the opposite of this. It is a temptation that often comes to us *sub angelo lucis*, disguised as good, and ultimately has its root in 'the rejection of the cross and the cultivation of self instead of the greater glory of God'.[83] 'This stifling worldliness can only be healed by breathing in the pure air of the Holy Spirit who frees us from self-centredness cloaked in an outward religiosity bereft of God.'[84]

---

81 See Rom 12:2.

82 See Phil 2:1–11.

83 Diego Fares SJ, 'Against Triumphalism and Spiritual Worldliness', *La Civiltà Cattolica* (English edition), 10 January 2022. See also G. Uríbarri, 'Tres cristianismos insuficientes: emocional, ético y de autorrealización: Una reflexión sobre la actual inculturación del cristianismo en Occidente', *Estudios Eclesiásticos*, 78 (2003), pp. 301–331. Both highlight the problems of a Christianity without the cross.

84 Pope Francis, *Evangelii Gaudium* (Vatican: The Holy See, 2013), 97, www.vatican.va/content/francesco/en/apost_exhortations/documents/papa-francesco_esortazione-ap_20131124_evangelii-gaudium.html

Moment Six:

Some Theological Points

An important and very topical challenge of the spiritual crisis we are living through is that *ordinary* knowledge is not enough; we need *extraordinary* knowledge. The established principles, the habitual practices, the accumulation of experience that constitute the various traditions are no longer sufficient, perhaps because our traditions have distanced us from dynamic nature of Tradition (cf. Mk 7:8–13). We have to continually retrace our steps back to the source of Tradition and to recover its most authentic channel.

At a juncture like this one, as often before in the two-thousand year history of the Church, we need *extraordinary* knowledge. We need to receive the renewing Word that comes from on high and to put it into practice, collaborating with God's action. We need to listen to and welcome the Word that comes from outside, one that establishes a new way while at the same time linking us to the origin of our Tradition in order to recover it, uniting its different elements and at the same time updating it. It is essential to listen to the Spirit who creates harmony and who continually brings us back to Christ.

The Church does not look to the world for the extraordinary knowledge it needs, for it knows this would be a merely self-referential path to take. Rather, it knows that this extraordinary knowledge at this moment in history can come only from allowing itself to be led by the Spirit of the Lord. The Church is in listening mode. And to do this, it has reached back to valuable elements of its Tradition: the synod, discernment and spiritual conversation.

Synod, discernment, discernment in common and spiritual conversation – we think it should be clear by this point in the book – are neither a recent fad nor the preserve of any one group within the Church. They are the ways in which, from the beginnings of the Church, Christians personally and as a group have built communion. It is also how they have sought to conform to God's will in making decisions affecting an individual, a community or a church group. It is how they have sought to direct their lives, not merely by the accepted moral standards of the society of the day, but by seeking to be led by God.

The synod, walking together and together dealing with problems, goes back at least to the wilderness wanderings of the people of Israel. In the Church, meanwhile, there has been no shortage of experiences of walking together and seeking together the will of the Lord, starting with the election of Matthias or the so-called Council of Jerusalem (Acts 15). Today, at this time in its history, the Church did not want to turn this process into a forum for experts but to call the whole Christian people to this journey of listening and discernment, giving expression to the Church as the body of all the baptised, according to the understanding that unfolded at the Second Vatican Council.[85]

The instrument of discernment is present in Scripture. Jesus teaches discernment to his own. We also find it in the Desert Fathers from the first centuries of the Church when, to a large extent in the West, it began to be formally set down, at least from the time of Cassian. There have been less complicated times when a way of proceeding is peacefully followed, and there is less talk of discernment. But in times of crisis, faced with various directions to follow, discernment has always reappeared in the Church.

When discernment is practised by a discerning group or community, conversation in the spirit, structured in one way or another, has been associated with processes of communal discernment.

This way of operating raises for some a series of questions. Are the rules no longer given, and is the path to follow no longer clearly indicated?

---

85 *Lumen Gentium* (Vatican: The Holy See, 1964), 12, www.vatican.va/archive/hist_councils/ ii_vatican_council/documents/vat-ii_const_19641121_lumen-gentium_en.html

Is it not enough for a good discernment to apply the rules and make a common-sense choice? Is it not pretentious to want to choose God's will? Why should we want all to participate when there are so many people who do not live the Church as much as those who are dedicated to it, such as the clergy and religious men and women? Does this not create confusion among ordinary people? Are we not introducing division into the Church, leaving our communion wounded? What guarantees does this path offer? Is it not too complex, and in the end won't it be the most powerful media who set the agenda of the synod or dictate its conclusions? Is there not a big risk that the Church will be confused and set adrift?

Discerning beyond general norms and givens

Jesus warned us that not everything had been said; or, at least, that we could not understand everything: 'When the Spirit of truth comes, he will guide you into all the truth' (Jn 16:13). Listening to the Spirit and, therefore, discernment, is indispensable in our life as believers, lest we miss something important of the truth.

Theologians have discussed discernment in two different ways. For some, discernment is a simple matter of common sense and prudence, plus a certain psychological awareness, which allows us to apply established general principles to concrete situations.[86] For others, it is a way of knowing beyond common sense and the deduction from general principles, one that allows each person to discover their concrete purpose: not as a mere deduction from general principles, but as an inspiration of the Spirit who is at work in our lives.[87]

When it comes to important decisions facing a community or the life of the Church, we can see as normal what is presented to us in each situation, taking it as read. This could be understood as the sum of possibilities at hand, whether in law or the prevailing morality or knowledge of the objective order of things, of human beings or of history. Choosing would be therefore a matter of making a choice from what in effect is already present.

86 Cf. Juan Luis Segundo, *El hombre de hoy ante Jesús de Nazaret* (Madrid: Cristiandad, 1982), pp. 719–735.
87 Cf. Karl Rahner, *Lo dinámico en la Iglesia* (Barcelona: Herder, 1963), pp. 102–104.

But if Christian choosing were like that – objective reasoning, deductions from general principles, selecting from the possibilities at hand – it would not do justice to the manifestation of God's goodness and justice in Christ, who recreates the possibilities of what is human and real. When Paul prayed for his Ephesian community, he asked they be given 'a spirit of wisdom and revelation' so that 'the eyes of your heart' be enlightened in order to know 'the hope to which he has called you' (Eph 1:17–18). That call is the result of Christ's resurrection, which is a power 'far above all rule and authority and power and dominion' (Eph 1:21).

It is not a question of Christians thinking apart from our human condition or the world we live in but of embracing the newness of the horizons of humanity brought about by the death and resurrection of Christ. Paul advises us not to conform ourselves to this world but rather to 'be transformed by the renewing of your minds, so that you may discern what is the will of God – what is good and acceptable and perfect' (Rom 12:2). The renewal that has come leads us to probe what God wants from us in a more personal way: not to be conformed to what is at hand, but to scrutinise the possibilities and the promise of what we have been given, so that we may reclaim it.

Not always but sometimes it happens that in discernment we transcend what is taken for granted, what is already there. It is characteristic of God to enter and leave the soul, or to move it, without a prior cause or object.[88] It is proper to the Creator to act with his creature and to continue to create. That touch of the Lord transcends the context, goes beyond what is given. Then it will need to be embodied in something concrete: something we have already been given, perhaps, or what broadens the possibilities of what is given by bringing to it something new.[89]

'And they shall all be taught by God'

In seeking to discern and to lead our lives according to the Spirit, we find that God has always wanted to communicate – self-communicate – to human beings, and to do so personally: 'Long ago God spoke to our ancestors in many and various ways by the prophets, but in these last days he

---

88 *Spiritual Exercises*, 330.
89 Cf. A. Tornos, 'Fundamentos biblio-teológicos del discernimiento', *Manresa*, 60 (1988), pp. 319–329.

has spoken to us by a Son, whom he appointed heir of all things, through whom he also created the worlds' (Heb 1:12–2). From the prophets there opened a hope raised by the promise that God would imprint his law on our hearts: 'no longer shall they teach one another, or to say to each other, "Know the Lord", for they shall all know me' (Jer 31:34).

God communicates himself and does so to *all*. Jesus picks up the promise enunciated by Isaiah when he says, 'and they shall all be taught by God' (Jn 6:45; Is 54:13). We are all hearers of the Spirit, hearers of the Word, disciples of God. This means that each of us has received something personal and unique from the Spirit, something that contributes to the development of the Church. To deny anyone participation is to lose something of what God gives to his Church. *Participation* is one of the three key words of the synodal assembly, alongside *communion* and *mission*.

We asked earlier if calling *everyone* together and wanting to listen to *everyone* might not create chaos and endanger communion. Against this we must affirm that it could not be otherwise than by calling everyone together, for 'all the baptised, whatever their position in the Church or their level of instruction in the faith, are agents of evangelisation, and it would be insufficient to envisage a plan of evangelisation to be carried out by professionals while the rest of the faithful would simply be passive recipients'. Pope Francis went on to say that the *sensus fidei* (on which, more shortly) 'prevents a rigid separation between an *Ecclesia docens* and an *Ecclesia discens*' – that is, the Church that teaches and the Church that learns – 'since the flock likewise has an instinctive ability to discern the new ways that the Lord is revealing to the Church'.[90]

Everything in our day, starting with the Second Vatican Council, urges us to a new, real and effective participation of all the baptised in the Church. *Lumen Gentium* showed a new face in moving from the pyramid Church of Christendom to a vision of the Church as the People of God[91]

---

90   Pope Francis, 'Address at the Ceremony Commemorating the Fiftieth Anniversary of the Institution of the Synod of Bishops', 17 October 2015, www.vatican.va/content/francesco/en/speeches/2015/october/documents/papa-francesco_20151017_50-anniversario-sinodo.html, quoting *Evangelii Gaudium*, 120.

91   *Lumen Gentium*, 9.

and universal sacrament of salvation.[92] The logic of the layout of the first three chapters of this constitution of the council already points in this direction: Mystery (I), People of God (II), Hierarchical Constitution (III). What this reveals is that in the historical design of salvation the hierarchy is at the service of the People of God.[93] In this sense, synodality expresses the status of the subject that corresponds to the whole Church and to all in the Church.[94] All the baptised share in the one priesthood of Christ and receive the charisms of the Holy Spirit.[95] Therefore, in the prophetic, priestly and kingly People of God, all are active subjects, disciples and missionaries, called to proclaim and bear witness to the Gospel.[96]

To consider in the second chapter the Church as the People of God and then, in the third chapter, to deal with its structure is little short of a revolution. It is not accidental but is a real turnaround in the vision of the Church and in its desire to overcome clericalism. The very content of both chapters was a great novelty that recovered the tradition of the Church, moving from a Church understood as a pyramid structure to a Church founded on the participation of all Christians in the threefold function of Christ as priest, prophet and king.

When the Second Vatican Council proposed an ecclesiology that pivots on baptism, giving priority to this sacrament that is common to all Christians, it naturally opened the door to new possibilities for understanding the life and exercise of ministry in the Church and a greater participation of all the faithful in the development of the Church. It is worth recalling the theological axiom enunciated by St Cyprian that 'what concerns each and every one must be discussed [approved] by all'. This was how it was in

---

92   Cf. *Lumen Gentium*, 1, 48, 29; *Gaudium et Spes* (Vatican: The Holy See, 1965), 45, www.
     vatican.va/archive/hist_councils/ii_vatican_council/documents/vat-ii_const_19651207_
     gaudium-et-spes_en.html; *Ad Gentes* (Vatican: The Holy See, 1965), www.vatican.va/
     archive/hist_councils/ii_vatican_council/documents/vat-ii_decree_19651207_ad-gentes_
     en.html, 1, 5.
93   *Lumen Gentium*, 27.
94   *Lumen Gentium*, 31.
95   *Lumen Gentium*, 1, 12.
96   *Lumen Gentium*, 10; cf. Santiago Madrigal SJ, *Conferencias episcopales para una Iglesia
     sinodal* (Santander: Sal Terrae, 2020), p. 134.

the early centuries of the Church.[97] And in order that it may be so in our days, in order to deepen communion, the practice of spiritual conversation and discernment in common is of great importance.

In noting how, in the conversation in the Spirit, we participate on an equal footing, in no way do we wish to put on the same level let alone eliminate the various charisms, differences and even hierarchies that exist or can exist in the Church. We are simply expressing that there comes a time in the communal discernment process when we all listen to the Spirit and take part on an equal footing as 'disciples taught by God'.

We are equal and we are different

In walking together and listening to each other, we have to combine the fact that we are equal yet different. Synodality seeks to enable the integration of the gifts and voices of the People of God, the College of Bishops and the successor of Peter in an 'ecclesiological vision [that] invites us to articulate synodal communion in terms of "all", "some" and "one".'[98] This is not about lumping together and levelling everything in an homogenous egalitarianism that erases differences, in which we would be not only 'equal' but also 'the same'. We are not ignoring the diversity of charisms in the Church, but seeking to walk together with those differences that enrich the Church. Let us not forget that in the Gospel it is the women who are the first to bear witness to the resurrection of the Lord and to announce it to the apostles (Lk 24:9). And it is the beloved disciple rather than Peter who first recognises the presence of the risen Lord by the lake (Jn 21:7).

In the very first words of the newly elected pope at the beginning of his pontificate – very likely influenced by the diagnosis made in the cardinals' meetings prior to the conclave, from which the pope

---

97 C. M Galli, 'Líneas teológicas, pastorales y espirituales del magisterio del papa Francisco', *Medellín*, (2017), pp. 95–158 (p. 134). In his 50th anniversary synod speech, Pope Francis described the axiom *Quod omnes tangit ab omnibus tractari debet* as 'a principle dear to the Church of the first millennium'.

98 International Theological Commission, *Synodality in the Life and Mission of the Church* (Vatican: The Holy See, 2018), 64, www.vatican.va/roman_curia/congregations/cfaith/cti_documents/rc_cti_20180302_sinodalita_en.html. See also C. M. Galli, 'Líneas teológicas', and Rafael Luciani, 'El reto del tercer milenio: una Iglesia en clave sinodal', talk given to Academy of Catholic Leaders, 11 March 2023.

himself acknowledges having taken the programme for his pontificate – Francis referred to the journey together: 'Now we begin this journey, bishop and people ...' He used the word 'journey' three times in his speech. It is clear that Francis has sought to understand the hierarchical ministry in the light of the ecclesiology of the Second Vatican Council as a true service of self-giving love to the People of God:

> Journeying together – laity, pastors, the Bishop of Rome – is an easy concept to put into words, but not so easy to put into practice ... Synodality, as a constitutive element of the Church, offers us the most appropriate interpretive framework for understanding the hierarchical ministry itself. If we understand, as St John Chrysostom says, that 'Church and synod are synonymous', inasmuch as the Church is nothing other than the 'journeying together' of God's flock along the paths of history towards the encounter with Christ the Lord, then we understand too that, within the Church, no one can be 'raised up' higher than others.[99]

In his apostolic exhortation *Evangelii Gaudium*, Francis also introduces and nuances the idea of the synodal path, when, referring to the bishop, he notes how 'he will sometimes go before his people, pointing the way and keeping their hope vibrant. At other times, he will simply be in their midst', while 'at still other times, he will have to walk after them, helping those who lag behind and – above all – allowing the flock to sniff out new paths'.[100] What is more, the pope entrusts to the bishop the task of encouraging and developing 'the means of participation proposed in the Code of Canon Law, and other forms of pastoral dialogue, out of a desire to listen to everyone'.[101]

---

99 Pope Francis, 'Address at the Ceremony Commemorating the Fiftieth Anniversary of the Synod'.
100 **Translator's note**: my translation of the pope's words. The official Vatican translation renders it as 'allowing the flock to strike out on new paths', which fails to capture the pope's reference to the flock's *olfato* or sense of smell, that is, to its capacity for discovering those new paths.
101 Pope Francis, *Evangelii Gaudium*, 31.

Communion and mission

As has been said already, spiritual conversation geared to communal discernment is a privileged way indicated by the synod secretariat itself, one that allows us to participate in the life of the Church with a view to strengthening *communion* and renewing *mission* by listening to the Spirit. The Second Vatican Council and papal documents not only stress the participation of all, but see it as the basis of an ecclesiology of communion, which is referred to as a gift of the Holy Spirit: 'The Church, which the Spirit guides in way of all truth and which he unified in communion and in works of ministry, he both equips and directs with hierarchical and charismatic gifts and adorns with his fruits.'[102]

From the beginning of this synodal journey, the importance of communion has been stressed throughout the process. For an ecclesiology of communion, the Eucharist is fundamental, for it constitutes the assembly in the Body of Christ present in the Church. Trinitarian communion is regarded in this ecclesiological development of synodality as its 'source', 'shape' and 'goal'. The Holy Spirit is seen as moving us in a natural way towards a synodal understanding of the Church, as one who enlightens and enlivens this journeying together as brothers and sisters. And that same spirit, who is the originator of communion (2 Cor 13:13), is also the protagonist of synodality. Which is why we can say that synodality is inherent in the very nature of the Church understood as communion.

The council also directed us to a renewal of the Church's mission, encouraging us to respond to new circumstances with the ever new and timely message of the Gospel. It invited the Church to be attentive to 'the joys and the hopes, the griefs and the anxieties of the men of this age, especially those who are poor or in any way afflicted'.[103] To renew this mission and to sharpen our attention, the synod invites us to a communal discernment, an attentive and courageous listening to the 'sighs too deep for words' (cf. Rom 8:26), which opens a way through the cry – explicit but also mute – that rises from the People of God: 'to listen to God, so that with him we may hear the cry of his people; to listen to his people

---

102 *Lumen Gentium*, 4.
103 *Gaudium et Spes*, 1

until we are in harmony with the will to which God calls us'.[104]

The participation of all is also important for the renewal of the Church's mission, because 'the faithful are able ... to sense what Pope Francis has called "new ways for the journey" in faith of the whole pilgrim people. One of the reasons why bishops and priests need to be close to their people on the journey and to walk with them is precisely so as to recognise "new ways" as they are sensed by the people. The discernment of such new ways, opened up and illumined by the Holy Spirit, will be vital for the new evangelisation.'[105]

How can we be sure that we are not mistaken?

This is not a good question. There is something pharisaic about it. God is never bound by our concepts or decisions. God is always God. But we know that he does not hide from those who seek him with humility and a sincere heart. Discernment is a human method of seeking God's will. God and his will are absolute; the way we formulate these is second-best, expressed in the human way. Our personal or group discernments are not infallible. We can never 'be sure' that we have grasped the truth in our hands; rather, the truth grasps us. What we have is second-best, not absolute. God alone is absolute.

It is only by walking together and expressing our faith together that we do not err. This is what a couple of theological concepts recently rescued by the International Theological Commission teach us. They are two close relatives of discernment that will be of great service in a more synodal Church, enabling us to move forward with confidence: the *sensus fidei* and the *sensus fidelium*.[106] In the journey together that is proposed to us, listening to the Spirit and listening to each another, God's holy people are revealed to be infallible *in credendo*, in their believing:

---

104 Pope Francis, 'Address at the Prayer Vigil for the Synod on the Family', 4 October 2014, quoted in International Theological Commission, *Life and Mission*, 114.

105 International Theological Commission, *Sensus Fidei in the Life of the Church* (Vatican: The Holy See, 2014), 127, www.vatican.va/roman_curia/congregations/cfaith/cti documents/ rc_cti_20140610_sensus-fidei_en.html

106 **Translator's note**: the *sensus fidei* is the instinct of faith, while the *sensus fidelium* is the instinct of the faithful. The two can be put together: the *sensus fidei fidelium* is the faithful's instinct of faith.

In all the baptised, from first to last, the sanctifying power of the Spirit is at work, impelling us to evangelisation. The People of God is holy thanks to this anointing, which makes it infallible *in credendo*. This means that it does not err in faith, even though it may not find words to explain that faith. The Spirit guides it in truth and leads it to salvation. As part of his mysterious love for humanity, God furnishes the totality of the faithful with an instinct of faith – *sensus fidei* – that helps them to discern what is truly of God. The presence of the Spirit gives Christians a certain connaturality with divine realities and a wisdom that enables them to grasp those realities intuitively, even when they lack the wherewithal to give them precise expression.[107]

The *sensus fidei* is a kind of faith instinct that believers possess. It is like an intuition about the right path to follow in the midst of the uncertainties, difficulties and ambiguities of historical reality. It endows the faithful with the capacity to listen in a discerning way to what human culture and knowledge are saying and to grasp in them the seeds of the Word. God's holy people are 'a people of prophets' for its *sensus fidei* is 'a kind of "spiritual instinct"' that allows them to *sentire cum Ecclesia* and to discern what conforms to the apostolic faith and to the spirit of the Gospel'.[108]

The *sensus fidei* prevents a rigid separation between the Church that teaches (*Ecclesia docens*) and the Church that learns (*Ecclesia discens*), because of the spiritual capacity of the Christian people to find new ways that the Lord always opens to his Church – its 'sense of smell'.[109] The *sensus fidei* is also expressed in various forms in Catholic popular piety.[110]

While the *sensus fidei* has a more personal dimension, the *sensus fidelium* points to the capacity of the whole People of God to discern together the truth of the faith and to pass it on. It looks not just to the past but is a

---

107 *Evangelii Gaudium*, 119, drawing on *Lumen Gentium*, 12.
108 Pope Francis, 'Address of Pope Francis to the Members of the International Theological Commission', speech, 6 December 2013, www.vatican.va/content/francesco/en/speech-es/2013/december/documents/papa-francesco_20131206_commissione-teologica.html
109 Pope Francis, 'Address at the Ceremony Commemorating the Fiftieth Anniversary of the Synod'.
110 International Theological Commission, *Sensus Fidei*, 110–112.

proactive and interactive process of discerning reality, and is the way the Church and all its members make their way through history.

The radical desire to listen that the Church is showing in this synodal process suggests that it wants to gather up all that God is giving us, all the manna, 'so nothing may be lost' (Jn 6:12).[111] And so no one may be left behind. Hence Pope Francis's insistence, reiterating the words of Pope Benedict, that 'the theologian must continually listen to the faith that is lived out by the humble and the little ones, to whom it has pleased the Father to reveal what he has hidden from the learned and the wise (cf. Mt 11:25–26)'.[112]

We cannot be naïve either in this process. In the same address to the theologians, the Holy Father made clear that 'the *sensus fidelium* must not be confused with the sociological reality of majority opinion'. Hence the importance of developing 'criteria for discerning authentic expressions of the *sensus fidelium*'.[113]

This way of understanding the People of God in its totality, journeying together with its diversity of charisms, places no small responsibility on the shoulders and in the heart of every believer. It involves listening to the Word of God and to the Holy Spirit, both alone and in solitude and through the other members of the Church, discerning and allowing themselves to be led by the *sensus fidei*. The instrument of spiritual conversation and common discernment will help this faithful people of God along the way. Now we can turn to the more practical aspects of how to do this.

111 The radical desire to listen in obedience to God's will is the theme running through Pope Francis's cycle of 14 weekly catecheses on discernment between 31 August 2022 and 4 January. See www.vatican.va/content/francesco/en/audiences/2022.index.html
112 Pope Francis, 'Address to Members of the International Theological Commission'.
113 Pope Francis, 'Address to Members of the International Theological Commission'.

Moment Seven:
Holding a Conversation in the Spirit

The *Instrumentum Laboris* proposes a basic outline for conversation in the Spirit that is represented in the diagram. As presented in the working document, the method involves three basic stages commonly known as 'rounds'.[114] Taking for granted a prayerful atmosphere and moments of prayer prior to each round, 'the first is devoted to each person taking the floor, starting from his or her own experience reread in prayer during the period of preparation. Others listen in the knowledge that each one has a valuable contribution to offer, and refrain from debates or discussions'.[115]

In the second round, prepared by silence and prayer, 'each person takes the floor: not to react to or counter what they have heard, reaffirming their own position, but to express what from their listening has touched them most deeply and what they feel challenged by most strongly. The interior traces that result from one's listening to sisters and brothers are the language with which the Holy Spirit makes his own voice resound'.[116]

The third round, 'again in an atmosphere of prayer and under the guidance of the Holy Spirit', is in some ways more complex than the previous ones: 'to identify the key points that have emerged and to build a consensus on the fruits of the joint work'. It is not a question of seeking

---

114 We should not imagine that merely applying a method, of whatever sort, will make the Spirit of God speak. The Spirit is always sovereign in the relationship. We cannot expect the methodology to work without the dispositions of the heart that we have presented in the previous pages. We arrange ourselves in the best way we know how, in humility, so that when and how the Spirit wills, he communicates himself to us.
115 *Instrumentum Laboris for the First Session*, 37.
116 *Instrumentum Laboris for the First Session*, 38.

The conversation in the Spirit

A dynamic of discernment in the synodal Church

PERSONAL PREPARATION

By entrusting oneself to the Father, conversing in prayer with the Lord Jesus and listening to the Holy Spirit, each one prepares his or her own contribution to the question about which he or she is called to discern.

Silence, prayer and listening to the Word of God

«Taking the word and listening»

Each person takes turns speaking from his or her own experience and prayer, and listens carefully to the contribution of others.

Silence and Prayer

«Making space for others and the Other»

From what the others have said, each one shares what has resonated most with him or her or what has aroused the most resistance in him or her, allowing himself or herself to be guided by the Holy Spirit: "When, listening, did my heart burn within me?"

Silence and Prayer

«Building together»

Together we dialogue on the basis of what emerged earlier in order to discern and gather the fruit of the conversation in the Spirit: to recognize intuitions and convergences; to identify discordances, obstacles and new questions; to allow prophetic voices to emerge. It is important that everyone can feel represented by the outcome of the work. "To what steps is the Holy Spirit calling us together?"

Final prayer of thanksgiving

a common denominator or citing the points that most often came up. 'Rather, discernment is needed, which also pays attention to marginal and prophetic voices and does not overlook the significance of the points on which disagreement emerges. The Lord is the cornerstone that will allow the "construction" to stand and the Spirit, the master of harmony, will help to move from cacophony to symphony.'[117]

The process culminates in thanksgiving and praise. 'Whenever we encounter another person in love, we learn something new about God.'[118]

As the *Instrumentum Laboris* goes on to say, we need a certain flexibility in adapting structured conversation in the Spirit to specific circumstances.[119] In our journeying together we should not lose sight of how 'conversation in the Spirit has been accepted and sometimes "discovered" as providing the environment that makes possible the sharing of life experiences and the space for discernment in a synodal Church.'[120] But the groups that meet and the topics discussed are varied. They might be parish groups of people who know each other and are used to meeting, or groups whose members come from different geographical locations and do not know each other. They might be parish groups who want to check in with each other in order to prepare themselves better for their usual activities that have already been agreed on; or they might be groups that must make complex choices about their mission or important aspects of it, in which much of the life of the community is at stake. Or they might be groups seeking to grasp the situation of the Church in a particular place, trying to define together their own position; or groups that have to decide on issues that will shape the life of a community for a long time into the future, and who need 'to listen to the Spirit, who is the true protagonist, and to receive from him a mission.'[121]

Within this great diversity, we can of course also find groups of older people as well as groups of younger people; and groups with a lot of experience and familiarity with discernment, or groups with less or no

117 *Instrumentum Laboris for the First Session*, 39.
118 *Instrumentum Laboris for the First Session*, 40.
119 *Instrumentum Laboris for the First Session*, 41.
120 *Instrumentum Laboris for the First Session*, 34.
121 *Instrumentum Laboris for the First Session*, 34.

experience in this practice of together seeking God's will using this methodology.

In each case a prayerful atmosphere will be important, in order to discern the contribution each one makes, to attune one's own listening, and to pay attention to the interior dispositions mentioned previously. But the variety of situations will require the method to be adapted to the situation of the group. In this task of adaptation the role of the facilitators will be crucial in adjusting the conversation in the Spirit to the situation of each group, while always sticking to the essentials. Both the *Instrumentum Laboris* for the first session and the *Final Document* stress the value of their role and the priority that needs to be given now to the training of facilitators in order to grow as a synodal Church.[122]

The kind of introduction that is most appropriate will depend on the group that is gathering and the topic of the meeting. If those taking part do not know each other and will be working together for some time, it is worth taking some time over the introductions. Depending on circumstances, it might be appropriate for each participant to share the spiritual moment they are in as part of this introductory phase.

The same is true of the way the three rounds are organised. In some cases the conversation in the Spirit may be held not in order to make a decision but primarily to share and to get to know each other, in which case it would probably be enough to stick to the first two rounds only. In cases where difficult and complex decisions have to be made on which there is a wide range of opinions, it may be advisable to have not only the three rounds but also the double round that we saw being used in the deliberation of the first Jesuits.

On the other hand, the experience of synodal practice suggests that it is always really helpful to mark the transition from one round to the next with silence and brief moments of prayer in order to take in what is happening in the group, to recollect, to ruminate and to discern what is being heard.

Depending on how the conversation in the Spirit has been held – whether it has gone smoothly, or ended up as a discussion, whether affective or ideological attachments or ties have come to the surface – it can help at

---

122 *Instrumentum Laboris for the First Session*, 42; *Final Document*, 86.

the end to have a time of thanksgiving and review of what has been lived. Everything that happens in the conversation can work towards the good; we need eliminate nothing, but learn from everything (cf. Rom 8:28).

Throughout the three rounds we are engaged in discernment, both in what we share and in our opening to what we hear. But when the conversation is geared to making a decision, there is a special kind of discernment that has certain requirements that we will seek to clarify shortly. Decision-making is another phase that requires attention. When it comes, we cannot disregard the action of the Holy Spirit experienced in the conversation. We need to accept the grace offered to us, believe and make a decision accordingly.

(a): The introductory phase: the 'check-in'

Depending on the group and the circumstances in which it is meeting, it may be advisable to take stock before going into the three rounds and devote the initial part of the meeting to this. This way of beginning can help to start the meeting in a spiritual atmosphere. It may especially suit a group that has little experience of active listening and intentional speaking, in which case this phase may be worth taking particular care over, in order to improve the quality of the rest of the conversation.

This introductory phase, which some call a 'check-in', is designed to capture the disposition or inner state of each participant at the beginning of the meeting, which can be accompanied by a very brief explanation of why he or she feels this way.[123] This sharing can provide important insight into the situation of the person taking part in the discernment.

Certain situations that he or she may be experiencing outside the meeting may influence the conduct of the meeting or the nature of his or her participation. The introductory phase helps to reveal the frame of mind the participants are bringing to the meeting, or whether they are in a state of consolation or desolation. As well as showing what disposition participants bring to the meeting, it is a way of expressing that each person is welcome as they are now, and that each person's contribution is important.[124]

---

123 The term is used in Jesuits of Canada, *Toolkit*, pp. 10–13.
124 Jesuits of Canada, *Toolkit*, p. 11.

After an opening prayer, the facilitator might invite participants briefly to share how they are or feel at that moment, with questions such as 'How are you?' or 'How are you feeling as you come to this meeting?' Before the sharing begins, it is helpful to pause, giving time to those taking part to collect themselves.

If someone is experiencing particular difficulties, you can explore what is going on or, perhaps more sensibly, find the person outside the meeting in order to, if possible, listen and help them. Or, if an issue arises during the check-in that needs to be addressed during the meeting, it can be put on the agenda at the appropriate time.

This introductory phase might not be necessary or may simply not be possible in many groups, either because of the short time available for the process or because those in the group already know each other or even inhabit the same physical space, so that people are already aware of where the others in the group are. But where it can be done, it can make a big difference, affecting very positively the quality of the conversation in the Spirit that follows and the discernment. In many cases it provides valuable context to what each person shares.

(b): The three rounds

As we explained above, the basic outline of the conversation in the Spirit is that of the three rounds punctuated with moments of silence and prayer. The first round is the most straightforward, in that each person shares what he or she has experienced in prayer, whether feelings, emotions or reasons. The rest listen to him or her in an open way, with a willingness to alter their own perception or position in the light of what they hear. In this first round no one comments, not even in support of the one speaking. Some facilitators ask people to write down in advance what they want to share, to prevent them being conditioned by what people before them have said.

In the second round we share what has moved us from what we have heard. The Spirit can speak through others, and we have to be open to embrace what it wants to tell us. Here we have to apply what we have already said about active and vulnerable listening, keeping in mind the Ignatian presupposition that any good Christian has to be more ready to justify than to condemn a neighbour's statement.[125] If we are very attached to our opinion and find that it is not welcomed in the group, we may be tempted to repeat in the second round what we said in the first round, to try to sway the group. But we must not forget that the second round is about receiving that which is of the Spirit in what others have said. This is one of the great blessings of conversation in the Spirit, which takes us out of where we are, opens us up and enriches us. It moves us interiorly.

It is likely that, if it is a matter simply of taking the temperature of the group or sharing where we are, the second round is enough. There is nothing here to decide: we are sharing experiences and enriching each other, strengthening the bonds of the group and of communion. In this case, the conversation in the Spirit can end after the second round with a prayer of thanksgiving.

When there is something to decide, however, the third round is essential. In the second round the feeling of the group has been formed. At this point a more refined discernment becomes necessary, all the more so when the question to be decided calls for a more considered response.

Some say that discernment is too complicated. It is not complicated. In reality, what happens is the same as love. At its core, discernment is uniting ourselves to or attuning ourselves to 'the love that comes down from above', which, rather than being complicated, is delicate and needs care, sensitivity and finesse.

When we discern, we do so about things that are good or neutral. Along the way there is much to examine within ourselves in order to let ourselves be led by the good spirit. Yet the bad spirit sometimes consoles, acting as an angel of light (Lucifer). So we have to distinguish true from false consolation. To do this, it is helpful to ask where it comes from and where it is leading us. It is important in this situation to analyse the course of our feelings and thoughts: the beginning, the middle and the end.[126]

When it comes to choosing, it is not enough simply to go with majority opinion.[127] And when we speak of reaching consensus, this can mean sev-

125 *Spiritual Exercises*, 22.
126 Pope Francis, 'General Audience', audience, 30 November 2022, 'the true consolation', www.vatican.va/content/francesco/en/audiences/2022/documents/20221130-udienza-generale.html, referring to *Spiritual Exercises*, 333.
127 Pope Francis, 'Address to Members of the International Theological Commission'.

eral things, as we have already seen. We are not talking about consensus as the common denominator of what the group thinks. It has to be a more settled consensus. What we think spontaneously is not the same as what we come up with after leaving behind our desire, self-love and self-interest. The former is often simply the narrative of the media that we follow or criteria that we have uncritically absorbed from the groups we belong to or admire. The latter is the result of weighing up different considerations and discerning interior motions, both our own and those of the group or community, and this is what we mean by a distilled consensus.

Some decisions are more complex or difficult, especially where there is a diversity of opinions and strong or conflicting ideological positions involving different interests or some other backstory. It may simply be that the issue at stake is more far-reaching. In these cases the inner dispositions will have to be more carefully considered, and a 'double round' may be needed, such as that used by the early Jesuits in their deliberation. To avoid falling into polarisation and the clash of opposed positions, it is very helpful to pass through the sieve of total availability to God's will. One day can be devoted by all those taking part to being willing to embrace A, sharing their feelings and their reasons or considerations in its favour. And then another day can be given over to embracing the opposite position, bringing their feelings and reasons or considerations in favour of B. This exercise will make us more inwardly malleable to accepting the Lord's will and the decision that is eventually reached.

(c): Discernment

In addition to the dispositions we have already looked at in moment 5, which are more interior, we can point out here some necessary procedural conditions for a discernment in common.

- *Personal prayer beforehand, during and afterwards.* Without a prayerful atmosphere, discernment is not possible. It is assumed that each participant has a personal prayer life because what they bring to the group is its fruit.
- *Unity of purpose and diversity of means.* The whole group seeks the same common good, e.g., to fulfil God's will. What needs to be decided is the means to achieve the end on which all agree.

- *Personal discernment.* A discernment in common becomes very difficult if those taking part have no experience of personal discernment.
  Discernment is about detecting the spirit that is moving us. In choosing, it is important that we are led by the right spirit and that each
  participant knows and purifies his or her own spiritual awareness.
  This is also a condition for spiritual conversation. What we bring to
  or pour into the conversation, and what we take from it, is in some
  way what we discern.
- *Times of silence and examination* will be very important throughout
  the processes. There should be space for recollection, for silence, for
  reflective examination – there can never be too much of these.
- *Clearly identify the point to be discerned.*
- *Have good information on the matter to be decided.* You can even invite
  someone to address the group who can clarify the topic in hand or
  offer relevant information on it.
- *Define clearly from the outset the methodology to be followed* so that all
  involved know what it is.
- *Make clear from the outset how the decision will be reached.* If a final
  decision is to be taken by the group, it is good to define the kind of
  majority required, for example whether it is to be decided by consensus or whether the decision will be taken by an authority after hearing
  from the group.
- *Pay attention to the spiritual harmony* such that there are neither vic-
  tors nor vanquished.

(d): The Examen[128]

Many unforeseen incidents can occur in the life of a group meeting for a
spiritual conversation, whether or not it is geared to decision-making. We
must not forget that we are gathered in the name of the Lord in order to
share in his action in our lives or to seek together his will, always in an atmosphere of mutual listening and communion. In spiritual conversation,
as in the spiritual life in general, nothing is to be discarded: 'there is no

128 **Translator's note**: although the authors will explain the term in this section, it is worth noting here that 'Examen' is the word used by St Ignatius in the *Spiritual Exercises* to describe
the 'examination of conscience', which is set out as a five-stage review to help us be aware
of graces received and refused. Cf. *Spiritual Exercises*, 43.

wastepaper basket'.[129] Everything can be deployed to the good (cf. Rom 8:28); there is nothing we cannot learn from.

One of the phases that will need to be carefully examined is the time of desolation in the group. It is important to detect it and to react accordingly. The usual signs of desolation are disturbance and darkness; a difficulty in seeing the way ahead; restlessness; lack of faith, hope and love; listlessness, sadness ... [130]

Because in desolation we read the past negatively, we might feel a call to change direction or abandon the process we are in. This is not the time to do this. The recommendation in this case is that 'one should never make any change but should stand firm and constant in the resolutions and decisions' taken prior to the desolation and to move against desolation.[131] But we can certainly make changes to *ourselves*: change our attitudes to better dispose ourselves: by more prayer, more meditation, more Examen.[132] It also helps to have patience, which has much to do with hope, for desolation is not forever: the Lord will give us consolation in his time.

In examining our consciences we have to see whether we are really doing what we should be doing: whether, when we should be praying, we really do pray or in fact check our emails; whether we are taking the process seriously, and so on. In other words, we need to see if we are being lukewarm, lazy or negligent because, perhaps, we think we already know it all and that this process is not going to offer us much. Here may be a cause of desolation. Desolation is also a time of learning; it can teach us that we do not control or manipulate God. It shows us that consolation is a gift, not something we can engineer or earn, and tests our willingness to proceed without rewards.[133]

The Examen is the place of our learning: to review what has happened to us and what we have experienced, the places where the Lord has led us and where we may have lost our way. At the end of a meeting it is helpful to do a brief Examen together, to give thanks for the experience and to gather the graces received; but also to identify attitudes that may have

129 This is the expression used by Adolfo Chércoles SJ in his talks.
130 *Spiritual Exercises*, 317.
131 *Spiritual Exercises*, 318.
132 *Spiritual Exercises*, 319.
133 *Spiritual Exercises*, 322.

been an obstacle to the group's progress in listening to the Spirit or to make us aware of something that happened: if the spiritual conversation went awry, say, or got sidetracked into a discussion.[134]

Some call this stage an 'evaluation', others 'review'. We prefer to keep the traditional name of Examen, which begins with thanksgiving to God. The Examen puts us in our rightful place: in gratitude, acknowledging what we have received. Rather than placing us at ground zero, as if we were responsible for our own creation, it treats us as recipients of graces that we have been given and which, in our welcoming them, bring us life. This is why it makes little sense to speak of evaluating, for this suggests a position of a certain superiority over what happens or over the graces received.

The Examen is also a moment of discernment whose subject matter is the progress of the conversation in the Spirit, namely to discover and to recognise the Lord's presence in it or the obstacles we have put in his way.

(e): The decisions

In meetings or pastoral gatherings it is often the case that, when principles are invoked – the centrality of the love of Christ, for example, or the importance of Christian virtues – and remain at the level of generalities, with nothing being actually decided, there will be agreement, a good atmosphere, fraternity and mutual understanding. Usually the conversation in the Spirit will proceed and develop smoothly – until the moment the principles begin to land. As people move to decisions and descend to the concrete, they are forced to move out from they are. At this point, when they must move ahead, accepting what perhaps was not in their plans, spiritual conversation can easily turn into a mere 'discussion'. At this point the nice atmosphere of communion and agreement can turn tense, and the distance between those taking part widens. And it can happen in this situation that subtly – consciously or unconsciously – decisions are boycotted, and the concrete steps previously agreed upon now cannot be taken.

God's gift is meant to bear fruit. The Word we receive is called to 'bring

---

134 A concrete way of carrying out this Examen or review can be found in the *Toolkit*, pp. 14–18.

forth and sprout', to provide 'seed to the sower and bread to the eater'. The Word we receive is meant to accomplish God's purpose for it (Is 55:10–11). Yet when it comes to putting it into practice, to give it concrete expression for the good of the Church, we can go aground. It may because of the temptation of gnosticism about which Pope Francis warns us: 'a purely subjective faith whose only interest is a certain experience or a set of ideas and bits of information that are meant to console and enlighten but which ultimately keep one imprisoned in his or her own thoughts and feelings'. Or it may the temptation of 'the self-absorbed promethean neopelagianism of those who ultimately trust only in their own powers and feel superior to others because they observe certain rules or remain intransigently faithful to a particular Catholic style from the past'. [135]

Faced with the difficulty of settling on decisions, we have to be attentive and, as Pope Francis says, recognise that 'realities are more important than ideas'.[136] Ideas can be glorious, but in times of fragility such as those which the Church is now living in many places, we need the humility to give up past glories and to welcome the gift that is being offered to us, even if it is not as it was in the past and not as we imagine in our fantasies. The Gospel teaches us to love the seminal, the little, the mustard seed, the widow's mite and to become aware of these.

Another aspect worth considering is that decisions do not conclude when they are formulated, but must be confirmed by discernment.[137] Time will be a key criterion: among the signs of confirmation is that the peace that the decision leaves behind lasts over time. Another sign is that the decision has been reached out of a place of gratitude rather than fear, leaving the heart thankful. Or when we feel that life clicks into place and the pieces fit together, when we sense that we are in the right place, simply and peacefully. Or we see that the choice we have made continues to keep us free and unburdened by disordered attachments. Normally choices that have not been well made have a certain stridency that sooner or later makes itself felt, revealing itself as it does so.

135 Pope Francis, *Evangelii Gaudium*, 94
136 Pope Francis, *Evangelii Gaudium*, 231–233. A model guide for communal decision-making can be found in the *Toolkit*, pp. 34–44.
137 Pope Francis, 'General Audience', audience, 7 December 2022, 'the confirmation of the good choice', www.vatican.va/content/francesco/en/audiences/2022/documents/20221207-udienza-generale.html

(f): *The facilitator or moderator*

Facilitating is about enabling the process, ensuring that the objectives of a meeting are met. In spiritual conversation, the facilitator has to ensure that the process flows and that the meeting remains focused on its goal.[138] This is how to ensure fruitfulness. The facilitator is an accompanier with an aptitude for listening, who maintains the tone and pace of the meeting. He or she makes sure that the participants listen attentively to each other, converse with each other as the steps of the methodology indicate and are attentive to what the Spirit may be suggesting to them. The facilitator can be more than one person. He or she assists as much as possible to make sure that all participants express themselves with quality and warmth. When the facilitator is part of the group, he or she also speaks and shares, although it is best for them not to go first.

He or she should be attentive to the time allotted for each of the rounds of the spiritual conversation, ensuring the short pauses between each round, while also monitoring the time for speaking that is available for each member of the group or discernment community. Experience tells us that it can be helpful for the facilitator to use the stopwatch on their mobile phone to keep track of how long each has spoken for.

It is an important quality of the facilitator to be free to set the ground rules for the smooth running of the meeting and to ensure all are familiar with the topic to be discussed. He or she should also not be afraid to interrupt when a person goes on too long and overruns the time limit and to redirect or refocus the participants if they have wandered off topic.

It is advisable to have a facilitator for the large group, if there is one, and other facilitators for the small groups. In the case of large groups working during the day in small groups, it is part of the facilitator's responsibility to lead the plenary or plenaries if the meeting is longer than one day. It also helps at the end of the day if the facilitators give time to share, review and gather up the experience of the groups during the day. This is a convenient way of adjusting the methodology and helping each other to improve the dynamics of the synodal meeting.

It is important to keep in mind the temptations that the facilitator must

---

138 A very clear and straightforward presentation of the role of the facilitator can be found in J. García de Castro, *La voz de tu saludo*, ch. 8, 8.2c.

avoid when accompanying the group. Some of the main ones are distract-edness, excessive deference, authoritarianism, protagonism, irresponsibil-ity, paternalism, moralism and over-protectiveness.

As we have already pointed out, the facilitator is a figure to whom the synod attaches great importance. For this reason, the working document encourages specific training for this service, which, moreover, is key to extending synodality in the Church.

Appendix:
Templates for Conversation in the Spirit

In this appendix we propose some guidelines for spiritual conversation for communal discernment. We go back over the suggestions for procedure and interior attitudes for spiritual conversation and discernment already covered. We do so because the aids in this section can be used independently of the rest of the text, although they will be better understood and applied with the content of the book thus far.

As has been already said, conversation in the Spirit can be applied in different ways, depending on the situations we find ourselves facing, but it is important not to neglect what is essential in the methodology. We also need to keep in mind differing needs and objectives as well as variables of time and of the kind of group involved (team, community, parish etc.). The guideline we are setting out here is general and straightforward and can be applied in a large variety of settings. As indicated at the start, it presupposes that everyone has previously engaged in prayer or prayerful reading on the specific point or topic to be addressed in the small-group conversation in the Spirit.

The role of the facilitator
It is best if the facilitator is chosen before going to the small groups, along with the one who will act as secretary. The practice in synods so far points to the importance of choosing someone well suited for this service. It is the role of the facilitator to help all taking part to feel welcome; to provide a safe space by reminding everyone to be respectful; to gently invite all to participate but without forcing anyone to do so; to make clear that what is said in the group is confidential; to take care not to dominate the group conversation nor allow anyone else to do so; to stress the need to

listen to and learn from others. Theirs is also the delicate task of timing the participants so that everything flows according to plan. With certain kinds of participants, an extra dose of courage and firmness from the facilitator may be needed. The role of the facilitator is important, which is why the *Final Document* calls for 'the formation of facilitators, whose contribution is often crucial to the process of discernment'.[139]

The role of the group secretary

The group secretary takes notes and captures what we can call the group consensus. But it is also their job to collect interesting or innovative topics or ideas that arise during the dialogue, even if they are not agreed upon; to keep a record of important moments; to ensure that their notes include enough information that there is an account of what took place, what was shared in the group and the direction the Spirit appeared to be pointing to. It is important for the secretary to stick to what happened and not add from their own perspective. Prior to the plenary session, it is a good idea for the secretary to discuss his or her notes with the facilitator.

Diversity

When it comes to forming small groups, experience suggests that the more diverse they are, the better; in other words, when they bring together men and women, young and old, lay people with religious, priests and bishops – all of them on an equal footing as sons and daughters of God who listen to his Word.

---

139 *Final Document*, 86.

I

Guidelines for Group Conversation in the Spirit (following Personal Prayer) [140]

Facilitator's introduction

The facilitator welcomes the participants and makes them feel at home. He or she says a short opening prayer, to which he or she may invite others. Depending on the group, he or she may encourage a quick introduction of each of the participants.

Then they give the following guidelines for the smooth running of the meeting:

• The importance of active, respectful and open listening.
• The possibility of using a symbolic object in personal sharing in order to better focus the group on the person speaking. While the participant has that object in their hand, they have the floor and no one else speaks until they finish and another participant asks for the object and takes the floor.
• What is shared is the fruit of what has been experienced in the Lord in the previous prayer time (inner motions, feelings, insights). There is no dialogue about anything else.
• Keep short periods of silent recollection between each sharing and between each of the rounds.
• Remember that in the sharings we are not giving a sermon, nor trying to convince others nor have our own view prevail.
• If there are questions, they should be asked only when something has not been understood and an explanation is requested.
• Make clear the importance of respecting the times specified for each personal sharing and for each round.
• Remind people of the importance of letting the heart speak rather than ideas.

---

140 These guidelines have been adapted in part from *Pautas conversación espiritual* by José de Pablo SJ, based on ESDAC (Spiritual Exercises for Apostolic Communal Discernment). See also *Toolkit*, pp. 21–24.

The rounds

First round (3–4 mins per person)

Each of the participants shares the fruit of their prayer (insights, emotions, thoughts, feelings) in respect of the topic or the questions posed. They do so freely and openly. The rest of the group takes part purely by their open, receptive and vulnerable listening, paying attention with their whole person to how the Holy Spirit acts in each sharing (without judging and setting aside their own opinion).

Second round (15–20 mins)

After a brief reflective silence following the previous round, each participant shares and reflects on what impressed them most from the first round. They can interact, but should maintain the spiritual tension. It is important to remember here that they should not add anything new but refer to what they heard in the first round. I can ask myself: What has impacted me most in what I have heard? What do I feel to be a common concern? Where do I experience harmony? What emotions or feelings have I become aware of? What ideas come to mind?

Third round (10 mins)

This is a less structured round than the previous ones. Participants reflect on what stirred within them and in the conversation and what affected them most deeply. They can ask themselves: What is the Spirit saying to us? How or where is it guiding us?

It ends with a brief thanksgiving.

Plenary (time depending on the number of small groups)

After the working small groups have met, there is a plenary session. The secretary of each group comes forward and shares the main points that have been raised. If there is a question or questions that have guided the small groups, that will be the subject to be shared in summary form.[141]

---

141 In the event of having various small groups, the recommended number in each group is between five and eight. If there are various groups, a general facilitator will be needed to accompany the process, both to oversee the plenary and to make it as fruitful as possible.

II
General Method for Discernment in Common[142]

Preparation

The person responsible calls a group together for a shared discernment. In this case, it may be the same person who facilitates and takes responsibility for the process. It could also be the person who, after listening to what the group has discussed, makes the final decision.

- The group of participants for the discernment is selected.
- The appropriate time and place are chosen.
- It may be better for someone else to lead the discernment process. It will be their responsibility to guide, set the times, organise how to work and to moderate the group.
- It is important to clarify from the outset how the final decision will be made (by group consensus, the existing authority, or other examples or ways).

Taking stock of the issue to be addressed

In an initial meeting, the participants should deepen their knowledge of the issue to be discerned. It will help the whole subsequent process if the greatest possible degree of objective information can be acquired on the subject beforehand without forcing the analysis in any direction.

- *Managing information*: texts to share, reports from experts, significant research on the point, in such a way that there is sufficient clarity on everything that is relevant.
- *Dialogue and contrast of views*: clarification, awareness of the possible diversity of opinions etc.
- *Analysis* of the known reasons for and against the different positions to be discerned in order to provide greater clarity.[143]

---

142 Taken from the Spanish Province of the Jesuits, *Discernimiento en común: una guía práctica* (2019), pp. 16–21, https://pedagogiaignaciana.com/biblioteca-digital/biblioteca-general?view=file&id=2816:discernimiento-en-comun-una-guia-practica&catid=8
143 This stage in the process may be longer or shorter depending on the topic and its importance.

Reflection and personal prayer

Participants take sufficient time to pray and reflect personally on all of the above. For this it may help to offer a passage from Scripture that bears some relation to what one wishes to shed light on. And some guidelines such as the following:

- Spend some time giving thanks for the presence of God.
- Consider the context (the parish, the community, the organisation, the group etc.) involved in this discernment that I am about to carry out with others.
- Ask for light and inner freedom so as not to be carried away by fears, prejudices, tastes, preferences etc.
- Respond in writing:
  (1) External and internal conditioning that I bring with me and that take away my freedom in approaching the issue in question.
  (2) What brings me light, peace, encouragement and hope in relation to the issue? Consider where this comes from and where it takes me.
  (3) What causes me unease, fear, doubt, discouragement or anxiety in relation to this issue? Consider where this comes from and where it takes me.
  (4) Name that to which I feel invited or called in relation to the topic.
- End with thanksgiving.

Group sharing following the three rounds of spiritual conversation

It is important to stress once again the importance of interior dispositions, as well as listening attentively, openly and vulnerably, in such a way that each participant gradually opens up to the feeling of the group and grasps God's will regarding the object of discernment.

- *First round.* Each participant shares his or her thoughts; the others listen in the ways previously mentioned. The idea here is to grasp the inner movements and what the group is being called to. No one intervenes, there is no debate, nor any responses or objections. The moderator ensures that no one exceeds the time allotted for each participation. Three or four minutes for each person would

99

be appropriate.

• *Second round.* Each participant shares what has most struck or resonated with them from what they have heard. This should be done in one or two minutes per person.

• *Third round.* The aim is to reach a final convergence, attempting to gather the fruits of the sharing, as far as possible. Depending on the subject and the circumstances, it is also important to pay attention to and gather up the other contributions, even if they do not point to a consensus.

Result of discernment

This will depend on how the decision is taken. In the case of an authority present there, that person will decide whether he or she has obtained the necessary elements to make a judgement, whether all that has been shared offers sufficient clarity and can complete the discernment process.

If it is the group that must make the decision, it will be the group itself that will judge whether it has obtained a sufficient degree of consensus. If so, the discernment can be closed.

If consensus has not been reached, it will be necessary to consider how to proceed further. Some of the possibilities are:

a. Let the issue rest and return to it at an appropriate time.

b. Gather more information if this is the reason for the difficulty in not reaching consensus.

c. Carry out a new process of reflection, personal prayer and group sharing.

III
Brief Outline of the General Method of Discernment in Common

Preparation
Select the group that will participate, choose the time and place, indicate the person who will lead the discernment, indicate how the decision will be made. Take stock of the reality of the situation or question at issue. You could make use of:
- information from an expert, who can answer questions;
- dialogue and debate between different positions;
- analysis of reasons for and against.

Reflection and personal prayer
Spend sufficient time responding in writing to the following (or similar) questions, and then share the answers in the group (this is primarily a listening exercise):

a) What external or internal constraints take away your freedom?

b) What gives you light, peace, courage, hope in the face of this issue? Consider where what you feel or think comes from and where it leads you.

c) What causes you uneasiness, fear, confusion, discouragement? Consider where what you feel or think comes from and where it leads you.

d) What do you believe God is right now calling us to do?

The rounds
First round: sharing of answers. Each participant shares his or her written answers, inner motions and calls.
Second round: shorter, sharing the echo of what has been heard.
Third round: a single phrase or word that summarises the fruit of the sharing.

Result of the discernment

Assess whether sufficient clarity and convergence have been reached. If not, further discernment is needed.

IV
A Particular Method for Making a Decision[144]

This is a methodology that requires fair amount of preparation and effort on the part of the group. It is oriented towards discernment and decision-making. It is usually used in case of important decisions.

Preparation[145]
Two issues need to be clarified: a) The method to be followed and b) the precise object of the deliberation.

(a) *The way of proceeding* and how the decision will be reached are explained. This should be done by the person responsible for the process, the one who calls together the group for a common discernment; but it is best if the deliberation is moderated by someone outside the group and the convening authority. But this will depend on the issue at hand and the circumstances. Sometimes it is not necessary to invite an external moderator. What should be explained is what is being sought and what will happen if unanimity is not reached: on the synod of bishops, for example, a majority of two-thirds is needed for a proposal or text to be approved. During this process all communication will be in common, avoiding an exchange of opinions on the topic to be discerned.[146]

(b) *The object of the deliberation* and the decision must be clear and the group given all necessary information to be able to decide.[147] The object of the deliberation should be one only, not two or

---

144 Spanish Province of the Jesuits, *Discernimiento en común*, pp. 21–27.
145 Not all groups are equally ready to undertake this kind of deliberation. Preparation (in advance or soon before) will be done according to the needs of each group. The preparation could be by way of a talk, reading, dialogue or sharing.
146 Each of those taking part listens only to God, to themselves and to the group when it gathers. In this way you encourage the flow of the internal motions, as well as avoiding all possibility of outside influence and pressure. This is easier when all the participants are in the same place at the same time, not engaged in their routine occupations.
147 If some information is withheld, known only to some but not others, then clearly there can be no common discernment.

more alternatives. Depending on the complexity of the issue, more or less time, clarification and some discussion may be required.

The Steps[148]

(1)Presentation to the group of the topic of the deliberation. Once the method and the objective of the deliberation have been agreed, it helps for the participants to share their personal views on it.

(2) Prayer and reflection to bring to light the motions and reasons 'against' the proposal. Afterwards these are written down. It helps if each participant inwardly accepts that this will be the result of the election and to look for reasons that support this conclusion.

(3) Sharing of the reasons 'against', contributing the fruits of the prayer time. There is no debate or dialogue, just listening. Time is allowed for everyone to take in all that has been heard about the reasons 'against'. A note is taken.

(4) Prayer and reflection on the reasons and feelings 'in favour'. It helps if each participant inwardly accepts that this will be the result of the election and to look for reasons that support this conclusion.

(5) Group sharing of what has been experienced 'in favour' of the proposal. There is no debate or dialogue, just listening. Time is allowed for everyone to take in all that has been heard about the reasons 'in favour'. A note is taken.

(6) Personal prayer in order for each to make his or her decision before the Lord based on what has been thought about, prayed over and heard. Each participant becomes aware of their own

---

148 These steps can be adapted or simplified according to the needs of the group and its familiarity with apostolic discernment in common.

'disponibility' and openness to seek what the Lord most desires for us.[149]

(7) In a further round, each person shares his or her decision. If there is unanimity, the common decision is accepted. If there is no unanimity, what has been pre-determined in point (a) above will prevail. A decision by consensus could also be sought.

(8) Confirmation of the decision. This is about the group taking personal prayer time to reflect on the process that was followed, in order to confirm the decision taken. Then there is sharing of the confirmations that people have found, the feelings and motions that confirm it.[150] Subsequently, the authority on whom the decision depends (in each case) accepts the result and proceeds according to what has been agreed.

149 **Translator's note**: English-speaking Jesuits normally translate the Spanish word *disponibilidad* by the unfamiliar term 'disponibility', because 'availability' or 'readiness' fails to capture the Ignatian notion of detachment needed freely to choose God's will. 'Disponibility' means freedom as far as possible from attachments, self-interest and external pressures; key to authentic discernment is to become aware of those areas where we may not be truly or sufficiently free. Cf. *Spiritual Exercises*, 179.
150 If needed – if, for example, the topic is very complex – the 'in favour' and 'against' round can be repeated.

V

Selection of Biblical Texts to Help Deepen the Work of the Groups

Jesus enters into conversation with many people on the road. He does so in many different circumstances and for different reasons: to attract them, to accompany them, to introduce them to prayer, to form them, to offer them mercy, to heal them ...

- John 1:36–39: One of the first encounters of Jesus with his disciples, who wanted to know where he lived. They remained in his home the whole afternoon conversing with him.
- Matthew 6:9–13: Jesus teaches his disciples how to pray, and does so with the Our Father, which includes a conversation with God.
- Luke 9:18–24: Along the way, in dialogue with his disciples, Jesus allows them to discover the newness of his person: that he has been sent, as Son of God.
- John 3:1–21: Nicodemus the Pharisee visits Jesus by night to learn more about his teachings. Jesus makes the most of it and converses with him about the need to be born again, from the Spirit.
- Luke 19:1–10: Jesus takes the initiative and chooses Zacchaeus to share a meal at his house, which leads to the tax collector's conversion.
- Matthew 15:21–28: The conversation with this Syrophoenician woman opens Jesus to a new reality. She helps him to change the understanding that until now he has had of his mission.
- John 4:1–42: Jesus' dialogue with the Samaritan woman helps her to experience her thirst and to discover the source of living water that dwells in him.
- John 11:7–16: Jesus shares with his disciples the desirability of going to the house of his friend Lazarus, who has just died.
- Luke 24:13–35: The risen Jesus meets two of his disciples who are

walking along, desolate, on the way back to their old lives. The conversation with the Lord allows them to recognise him alive among them, and they are filled with joy.

Jesus also meets resistance, attitudes that hinder or block:
- John 8:3–11: The passage about Jesus and the woman caught in adultery shows us how the Scribes and the Pharisees are not sincere and transparent in their encounter with Jesus. Their ideology armour-plates them against his loving offer to help them discover their sinfulness.
- Luke 22:24–26: Conflict is generated in the group when some people seek power or to be considered more important than others. Each one is focused on his own interests. Jesus shows them the way and the attitudes needed for communion.
- Mark 12:13–14: In Jesus' discussion with the Pharisees over the payment of taxes to Caesar, their falsehood and hypocrisy can be seen in their words.
- John 6:48–58: Jesus shares with those listening to him his identity as living bread come down from heaven, able to give life to the world. This produces deep hostility in those around him. The weight of tradition, the law, harshness of judgement – all prevent them from accepting him.

Mary's dialogues
- Luke 1:26–38: The angel Gabriel visits Mary and announces that she is going to conceive and give birth to the Son of God. Mary responds with questions and joyfully accepts the angel's message.
- Luke 1:39–56: Mary and Elizabeth converse happily as they experience God's compassionate and faithful action in their lives and in the lives of their people.

Paul's meetings in the community
- Acts 15:6: Paul and Barnabas are summoned to Jerusalem to deliberate with the apostles on the novel presence of Gentiles in the Church.
- 1 Corinthians 12:4–7: Paul speaks to us of the diversity of gifts and

the existence of a single Spirit that manifests itself for the common good of all. In the conversation in the Spirit, the Holy Spirit is the true protagonist.

- 1 Corinthians 12:12–26: Paul presents us with the image of the Church as a body with many parts.

God comes close to his friends

- Genesis 18:22–33: In this passage Abraham has a conversation with God about the destruction of Sodom and Gomorrah and intercedes to save the city.
- Exodus 3:1–15: Conversation between God and Moses. God speaks to Moses from a burning bush, reveals his name and entrusts him the mission of delivering the Israelites from slavery in Egypt.
- Job 38–42: These chapters narrate a series of conversations between Job and God in which Job asks questions and God answers him, revealing his greatness and wisdom.
- Malachi 3:16: Those who fear the Lord converse with each other and the Lord listens to them.

Key Sources

Pope Francis: Encyclicals, Exhortations

Evangelii Gaudium (The Holy See, 2013), www.vatican.va/content/francesco/en/apost_exhortations/documents/papa-francesco_esortazione-ap_20131124_evangelii-gaudium.html

Dilexit Nos (The Holy See, 2024), https://www.vatican.va/content/francesco/en/encyclicals/documents/20241024-enciclica-dilexit-nos.html

International Theological Commission

Pope Francis, 'Address of Pope Francis to the Members of the International Theological Commission', 6 December 2013, www.vatican.va/content/francesco/en/speeches/2013/december/documents/papa-francesco_20131206_commissione-teologica.html

Sensus Fidei in the Life of the Church (The Holy See, 2014), www.vatican.va/roman_curia/congregations/cfaith/cti_documents/rc_cti_20140610_sensus-fidei_en.html

Synodality in the Life and Mission of the Church (The Holy See, 2018), www.vatican.va/roman_curia/congregations/cfaith/cti_documents/rc_cti_20180302_sinodalita_en.html

Jesuit Sources

Michel Bacq & ESDAC team, Brian Grogan SJ (ed.), *Communal Discernment: A Lamp for Our Synodal Path* (Messenger Publications, 2024).

Ignatius of Loyola, *Personal Writings*, translated with introductions and notes by Joseph A. Munitiz and P. Endean (Penguin, 1996).

Michael Ivans SJ, *Understanding the Spiritual Exercises: Text and Commentary* (Gracewing, 1998)

Jesuits of Canada, *Communal Apostolic Discernment: A Toolkit*, https://bit.ly/3XMYRhV

Portal to Jesuit Studies, Boston College, 'The Deliberations of Our First Fathers (1539)', https://jesuitportal.bc.edu/research/documents/

Synod on Synodality
September 2021: *Vademecum for the Synod on Synodality*, www.synod.va/en/news/the-vademecum-for-the-synod-on-synodality.html

9 October 2021: Pope Francis, 'Address of the Holy Father Francis on the Occasion of the Moment of Reflection for the Beginning of the Synodal Journey', https://press.vatican.va/content/salastampa/en/bollettino/pubblico/2021/10/09/211009a.html

10 October 2021: Pope Francis, 'Homily of His Holiness Pope Francis at the Opening of the Synodal Path', www.vatican.va/content/francesco/en/homilies/2021/documents/20211010-omelia-sinodo-vescovi.html

October 2023: *Instrumentum Laboris for the First Session*, www.synod.va/content/dam/synod/common/phases/universal-stage/il/ENG_INSTRUMENTUM-LABORIS.pdf

October 2023: *Synthesis Report*, www.synod.va/en/news/a-synodal-church-in-mission.html

October 2024: *Instrumentum Laboris for the Second Session*, www.synod.va/content/dam/synod/assembly2024/il/ENG-INSTRUMENTUM-LABORIS-A4.pdf

November 2024: *Final Document*, www.synod.va/content/dam/synod/news/2024-10-26_final-document/ENG---Documento-finale.pdf

25 November 2024: Pope Francis, 'Note of the Holy Father Francis to

Accompany the Final Document of the 16th Ordinary General Assembly of the Synod of Bishops', https://press.vatican.va/content/salastampa/en/bollettino/pubblico/2024/11/25/241125k.html

Vatican II
Lumen Gentium (The Holy See, 1964), www.vatican.va/archive/hist_councils/ii_vatican_council/documents/vat-ii_const_19641121_lumen-gentium_en.html

Gaudium et Spes (The Holy See, 1965), www.vatican.va/archive/hist_councils/ii_vatican_council/documents/vat-ii_const_19651207_gaudium-et-spes_en.html

Ad Gentes (The Holy See, 1965), www.vatican.va/archive/hist_councils/ii_vatican_council/documents/vat-ii_decree_19651207_ad-gentes_en.html

Acknowledgements

We want to thank in particular the Holy Martyrs Spirituality Centre in Asunción and its Jesuit community, which welcomed us and encouraged us to begin this book. We also want to thank the deputy director of the St Ignatius Spirituality Centre in Salamanca, the secretary of the *Manresa* review, as well as John Dardis and the Discerning Leadership team who, from the other side of the Atlantic, shared key materials.

Thanks also are due to Graciela Amo, Raffaelle Lanzilli, Luis López-Yarto, José de Pablo and Gabino Uríbarri who read all or part of the manuscript and made pertinent comments. For the original Spanish edition we thank Grupo de Comunicación Loyola, in the person of Ramón Alfonso Díez Aragón, and for this English edition Cecilia West and her team at Messenger Publications, who provided everything needed for this publication. Our thanks also to Austen Ivereigh for his translation and valuable suggestions for updating our references to synodal documents. (The Spanish edition was published before the end of the Synod on Synodality, while this English edition comes out after its conclusion in October 2024.)